Financial Literacy

A Guide to Empowering Your Financial Future

(Business Finance Basics Entrepreneurs Must Know)

Zachary Olson

Published By **Simon Dough**

Zachary Olson

All Rights Reserved

Financial Literacy: A Guide to Empowering Your Financial Future (Business Finance Basics Entrepreneurs Must Know)

ISBN 978-1-7775324-4-4

No part of this guidebook shall be reproduced in any form without permission in writing from the publisher except in the case of brief quotations embodied in critical articles or reviews.

Legal & Disclaimer

The information contained in this book is not designed to replace or take the place of any form of medicine or professional medical advice. The information in this book has been provided for educational & entertainment purposes only.

The information contained in this book has been compiled from sources deemed reliable, and it is accurate to the best of the Author's knowledge; however, the Author cannot guarantee its accuracy and validity and cannot be held liable for any errors or omissions. Changes are periodically made to this book. You must consult your doctor or get professional medical advice before using any of the suggested remedies, techniques, or information in this book.

Upon using the information contained in this book, you agree to hold harmless the Author from and against any damages, costs, and expenses, including any legal fees potentially resulting from the application of any of the information provided by this guide. This disclaimer applies to any damages or injury caused by the use and application, whether directly or indirectly, of any advice or information presented, whether for breach of contract, tort, negligence, personal injury, criminal intent, or under any other cause of action.

You agree to accept all risks of using the information presented inside this book. You need to consult a professional medical practitioner in order to ensure you are both able and healthy enough to participate in this program.

Table Of Contents

Chapter 1: Understanding Financial Statements 1

Chapter 2: Balance Sheet 17

Chapter 3: Sample Cash Flow Statement 37

Chapter 4: Financial Statement Analysis 49

Chapter 5: Managing Working Capital ... 71

Chapter 6: Financial Literacy Glossary Of Terms 98

Chapter 7: Income Statement 120

Chapter 8: Awareness Of The Financial Literation 132

Chapter 9: Habits For Successful 137

Chapter 10: Steps To Get Rich 146

Chapter 11: Think Thoroughly Prior To Deciding On A Career 162

Chapter 12: Determinable Goals 171

Chapter 13: Give Yourself Time 175

Chapter 14: Consistency Is The Key To Success 180

Chapter 1: Understanding Financial Statements

The ability to comprehend and read financial statements is an essential ability to understand how companies work. As financial statements are an result of accounting, knowing them can help you understand the accounting. Understanding this knowledge will help to make you a more effective manager.

The ability to comprehend financial statements also helps in making better decisions on the stock market since it will allow you to gain valuable information from of the Annual Report or a 10K.

If you're an entrepreneur who is planning to business startup, understanding your financial statements is essential to the credibility of your business when meeting bankers, angel investors as well as Venture Capitalists.

Financial Statements

The accounting information is prepared in a systematic manner, which is then communicated as financial Statements. Financial statements are financial reports that contain accounting data. They are organised so that those who use financial statements have a reliable rapid, efficient, and comprehensive method of understanding and reading the activities of the company.

Two fundamental financial statements, the Balance Sheet as well as the income statement.

The interested parties must be aware of the accounting and financial activities that a company performs. The Statement of Balance Sheet and the Income Statement serve as an official document of financial transactions of a company. They are prepared in a systematic manner, as well as in a manner which is consistent and simple to comprehend once you have a good understanding of the structure.

Financial Statements offer an overview of financial statements and an overview of how the business is doing. They present a clear image that is quickly compared between businesses and different industries. Knowing how to interpret and analyse the Balance Sheet and Income Statement can be a good way to begin understanding the accounting and financial.

Financial statements are the ultimate outcome of accounting and bookkeeping. Consider financial statements as the endpoint or purpose of accounting and bookkeeping. If you are aware of what you're doing and what the intended audience and who the target audience is, you are able to make informed bookkeeping decisions. Once you are aware of the solvency, liquidity and capital structure of the company it is easier to make sound investments and financing decisions.

Financial statements contain the information needed for quick analysis and evaluation of the state of business. An understanding of the basics of financial statements provides an understanding of how to improve the effectiveness of bookskeeping and accounting records. The everyday activities of an organization are defined by the cash which is earned as revenue as well as the amount that goes out to cover expense, the amount that is reinvested as profit and the cash that's used to purchase operational assets and also the cash due. All it is about money. Financial statements allow you to follow the financial situation.

The document that evaluates the daytoday operations of cash in and cash out over a certain period that is timebound, is known as The Income Statement.

The Income Statement

The income statement can be summed up as the following: Revenues less expenses = Net income. The word "Net Income" simply refers to income (Revenues) net (less) of expenses. Net income is sometimes referred to as earnings or profits. Sometimes, Revenues can be referred to as Sales.

This concept is wellknown to you. The goal is always to make things more money than what they cost to produce. If you purchase a home, you expect it to rise in value and you will be able to sell it in the future at a higher price than what you originally paid. If you want to create the ability to sustain a business for the longterm it is the same principle that is applicable. There is no way to offer things cheaper than it require to produce and continue to operate for a long time.

Consider the income statement with regard to your financial situation. There are your monthly earnings usually the salary you receive from work. Your monthly income is applied on your expenses for the month including mortgage payments, rent or car credit, groceries, gasoline utility bills, clothing phones, entertainment and so on. We want to see our costs be lower than the income we earn.

As time passes, and as we gain time, we get better manage our financial situation and realize that we should not spend more than what we earn. It is our goal to have a little extra cash towards the end of each month to reserve and put away. The money we put aside and put aside is known as retained Earnings.

The money that we set aside can be invested with an the intention of reaping future rewards. It is possible to put money into bonds and stocks or mutual funds. Or we can invest in the pursuit of education in order to increase our opportunities for earning as well as working. It's the same kind of discipline for managing money which is used in businesses. It's a matter of the size. There's an extra zeros following the numbers in a big company's Income Statement, but the concept is exactly the similar.

This principle is applicable to every business. The majority of revenue comes from sales of services or products. Costs are expenses you incur in order to run your business such as salaries as well as raw materials, production procedures and equipment factories, offices as well as lawyers, consultants marketing, shipping and utilities. All that is left is your Net

Income, or Profit. Again: Revenues Expenses = Net Income. "Your Income needs to be more than your Outflow or your Upkeep is your Downfall." My mom would often say this. :)

Net income can be saved to ease the burden of any future business operations or deal with unpredictable events or to invest in equipment, new facilities as well as technological advancements. A portion of the earnings could be distributed to company shareholders who are sometimes referred to as stockholders or shareholders, in the form of dividends.

Sample Income Statement

The next page contains the sample income statement to help you understand the layout and presentation of the data.

JJC Corporation

Income Statement

For the Year Ended December 31, 2018

(In Millions of Dollars)

Revenues

Sales Revenues 2306

Service Revenues 1066

Total Revenues 3372

Expenses

Cost of Goods Sold Expense 1492

Selling, General, and Administrative Expense 983

Research & Development Expense 505

Interest Expense 54

Total Expenses 3034

Pre Tax Income 338

Income Tax Expense @ 22% 74

Net Income 264

The Income Statement can also be often referred to as "profit and loss statement" or "statement of revenue and expense." People in the business world often employ the term "P&L," which stands for Profit and Loss Statement. An executive is believed to be a person with "P&L responsibilities" if they manage an independent division in which they decide on the sales and marketing process, as well as personnel, product, expense as well as strategy. P & L responsibility is one of the primary duties of an executive that is to monitor the income net from expenses of a department, or for the whole organization and has direct control over the allocation of resources for the company.

The words "profits," "earnings" and "net income" all mean exactly the same thing, and can be commonly used in conjunction.

Keep in mind that: Earnings (revenue or sales) + Expenses = Net Revenue or Profit

Google the phrase "income statement" and you will find a variety of presentations and formats. It is evident that there's variation based on industry and business's nature but all of them follow these fundamental principles.

The Balance Sheet

The Balance Sheet may be summed up as Assets = liabilities + equity. This is known as the accounting equation. You should memorize the equation. The three segments of the balance sheet will give you an understanding of the company's assets (assets) and has to pay (liabilities) in addition to the value of capital invested by shareholders or owners (equity).

The Balance Sheet provides a summary of the financial standing of a business at a specific moment in time. The balance sheet is prepared towards the end of each year or the quarter. The report summarizes the Assets, liabilities and equity.

Imagine how your house is funded as a basic statement of balance. The value of the asset is that of your home. The value is determined via appraisal or selling. The worth of your house is contingent upon the changes in market conditions. A appraiser considers recent sales that have occurred in the region and also adjusts for variations such as the addition of a bathroom or bedroom. The appraisal will also take into account the replacement value, what is the take to rebuild the home in the present cost of the materials and work. The mortgage liability is the balance, and the equity (in the case of this, we refer to the equity of the homeowner) is the amount that is the difference between these two.

If your house is worth more than what you owe, you are in positive equity. If your mortgage balance exceeds the worth of your home, you are in negative equity. This is often referred to as being "upside down" or "underwater".

The same principles are applicable to corporate balance sheets. If the assets are higher than the liabilities, the equity of shareholders is positive. If the debts are greater than the assets then the business is deemed insolvent. In this situation, a business declares bankruptcy.

Balance Sheet Presentation

The Balance Sheet is made up out of two elements. The assets are listed in a column before being tallied at the lower end of each column. Equity and liabilities are shown in a different column, with the liability section over the section on equity. The Equity and liabilities are combined separately before being grouped on the bottom. The columns may be presented as a stack and the Equity column is on at the top. Sometimes, these columns are displayed sidebyside with assets on the left hand side, and equity and liabilities on the right.

In the Liabilities and Equity show how the assets are funded. Totals for Equity and liabilities in the column to the right must be exactly the same as that of the Asset total on the lower lefthand column.

If a person talks about the lefthand portion of the balance sheet they're talking about assets. When they speak about the right part of the balance sheet it is referring to equity and liabilities.

To aid in comparison for comparison purposes, the numbers of the Balance Sheet numbers from the previous year's balance sheet are usually displayed alongside the numbers for this year. Keep in mind that the purpose of Statements of Financial Statements is to communicate the financial data with clarity and meaning in a in order for interested parties to quickly understand the overall situation and performance of the company.

In accordance with GAAP which is which is the U.S. accounting standard, the assets and liabilities are listed in sequence of their liquidity from the short to the long in the order you move down the list of items in every column. Cash is the asset with the highest liquidity therefore it's listed at the left side on the Balance Sheet. Debt that is longterm comes before those with shortterm debts, which are in the liability column. Equity is listed beneath liability column. Equity is listed above the Liabilities since shareholders hold rights to junior ownership of the corp's assets. In the event of liquidation or bankruptcy of the business, the funds taken from the sale of assets will be used first to repay the lender. The remaining money left after loans are paid is given to shareholders.

Outside of outside of the United States, the rest of the world displays things on the balance sheet in reverse order, starting from the lowest liquid to top and the highest liquid on the lowest. IAS stands for International Accounting Standards. International Accounting Standards are referred to as IAS.

Chapter 2: Balance Sheet

The following webpage will get the illustration of an example of a The following page provides an example of a Balance Sheet. Because they differ in design and content, it's an excellent idea to go through an instant look at examples. Google the word "balance sheet" and you will discover a myriad of examples, in different formats as well as presentations.

Balance Sheet

For Years Ended December 31

(In Millions of Dollars)

2017 2018

Assets

Current Assets:

Cash $ 500 771

Accounts Receivable 232 307

Inventory 420 420

Pre Paid Expenses 123 123

Total Current Assets 1275 1621

Property, Plant, & Equipment 747 747

Patents 711 711

Total Assets $ 2733 3079

Liabilities and Stockholder's Equity

Current Liabilities:

Accounts Payable $ 101 183

Accrued Liabilities 92 92

Notes Payable, Short Term 71 71

Total Current Liabilities 264 346

Bonds Payable 973 973

Total Liabilities 1237 1319

Shareholder's Equity

Common Stock 840 840

Retained Earnings 656 920

Total Shareholder's Equity 1496 1760

Total Liabilities & Stockholder's Equity $ 2733 3079

Assets and Depreciation

The assets are shown on the left right side on the balance sheet. They include liquid assets like the cash account, marketable securities and accounts receivable. These are known as current assets. A lot of assets are durable things like vehicles, equipment as well as factories and machines. They are referred to as Fixed Assets. The majority of the cash is put into fixed assets are bought. Fixed assets come with longevity that's substantially longer than the period when they are bought. This is why Fixed assets get capitalized according to their value and every year in their intended utile life, a part of their cost is deducted to determine how much the assets were "used" in that year. This is referred to as Depreciation. It gives a clearer view of the way that operations of an organization help to run the business and spreads out the cost over the course of its lifespan when it generates revenue. .

In the example above, if we purchased an item that we expect to last 5 years, for $50, we will record the purchase and record it on the Balance Sheet with a value of $50,000 as Fixed Asset. Every year, we'd reduce the amount by $10,000 the depreciation ($50,000/5). In the next year, the asset is shown at $40,000, $3000 in the 3rd year and in the fourth year and so on. The amount displayed in the balance sheet is that of the initial asset cost and less (net from) depreciation. Assets do not appear individually on the Balance Sheet, but are grouped together and presented in a single number.

This is the reason it is necessary to have a Cash Flow Statement. The $50,000 will lower our cash reserves at the beginning of the year, and this would appear in the section titled Investment on the cash flow statement. Every subsequent year that $10,000 expense for depreciation included in the Income Statement will be reflected on the Cash flow Statement as it was not cashbased expense during that year. It was merely an accounting expense that was used to be able to keep track of how much we assign towards our "use" of the machine.

Amortization has a similar structure to depreciation. The term "depreciation" is applied to tangible assets, while amortization is utilized for assets that are intangible like intellectual property such as trademarks, patents and other intellectual property. Amortization generally matches the asset's cost with the income it earns. Amortization could also mean the repayment of loans with a fixed repayment schedule, which included principal and interest by regular installments over the course of.

Such noncash transactions can be compensated within the Operation section in the Cash Flow statement an effort to make sure that it is accurate in reconciling the financial statements with the quantity of cash that is held at the bank. The Cash Flow Statement more in depth after we have talked about the other portion of the balance sheet, namely equity and liabilities.

Liabilities

These are claims on the assets of a company. These liabilities are classified as noncurrent or current. These are liabilities which will be due in the calendar year. They are the obligations that an company owes others. Together with Equity They are the way assets are used to fund. It could be a debt with a third party that is not related to the company like an institution, or employees who have earned wages and still not paid. The accounts payable, the payroll liability and note payables are some examples of liabilities.

Assets and liabilities can be categorised as either current or noncurrent. This distinction is important to the person who uses the financial statements for performing the ratio analysis. The book will cover ratio analysis as well as other analysis of financial statements strategies later in this book.

Current Liabilities

The current liabilities are those that which the business expects to pay off within 12 months from the date of the balance report. In addition, assets and income can be used to settle these obligations. It can be derived directly from the sales or current assets including cash held in your bank account.

The most commonly cited Current Liabilities include accounts payable. The amount a business has to pay its vendors for products or services, as well as to employees through pay, or to the tax authorities is classified as a present liability. Many companies have payroll obligations and associated payroll taxes meaning that the company is owed these taxes but hasn't yet been able to pay them. These types of obligations are recognized by the business and will be repaid in the short term.

The loans due less than 12 months from the date of balance sheet can also be considered present obligations. In the case of a company, it could require a temporary loan to pay for a payroll cost. It is usually designed as a line of credit (LOC) in the hope that the LOC will be paid for through the collection of accounts due or selling of stock.

The portion that is current on longterm notes due is considered to be as a liability for the present. Longterm notes will be returned in full following 12 months. But, you have to display the portion in effect, the one that will be reimbursed during the present operating period in the form of a present liability.

Unearned income is a class which includes the money that the business has earned from its customers but isn't yet earning through the process of completing it. The company expects to complete the work and earning revenue within 12 months from the date on the balance report.

Long Term Liabilities

Longterm or noncurrent obligations are those that the business isn't planning on paying off or settled within the 12 months after the date of balance sheet. The company uses debt to fund certain aspects of their business as well as assets. They are categorized as notes, loans or bonds that have principal and interest payments for the period of. The financing of a business involves the combination of equity and debt. The mix is referred to as the capital structure the business.

There are various types of longterm debt. They are distinguished by their claims on the company's assets. This is important when a business becomes bankrupt and files for bankruptcy. Senior debt is the first order to receive the profits of the disposal of assets. The junior debt must wait until senior debt is settled before receiving cash returned. This creates a higher risk for junior debt due to the higher likelihood of not being paid back in the case of a bankruptcy. Due to the higher chance of failure, the junior debts need a higher rate of interest to cover the additional risk.

A different financing option is Convertible Debt that can be transformed to stock.

Stockholders' Equity

In addition to liabilities, are considered as funding source for the assets of a company. Stockholders are the shareholders of the corporation. The corporate ownership is divided into stock and shares. The amount is determined by the number of shares which is authorized for the corporation when it was founded. The amount of shares authorized could be increased through an approval of the current shareholders. An organization raises money through selling stock shares. The quantity of shares that are issued and then sold is known as the Shares outstanding. It is 100% of the shares owned by the company. The amount of money that is raised and the quantity of shares that were issued are tallied and then displayed on the Equity section of the Balance Sheet.

The equity of the stockholder is the amount of assets reported in the balance sheet less the liabilities reported. In other words equity is the sum of the assets less liabilities. To understand this, take a look at the fundamental accounting formula:

Assets = Liabilities + Equity

Then rearrange it so that it solves the problem of Equity

Equity = Assets Liabilities

In the case of a business, there might be multiple types of stock that is issued. The different classes of stock be granted different rights in relation in relation to claims and voting assets, and consequently are likely to have different value. Simplely speaking, we can categorize stock into two categories that are called Preferred and Common.

Common Stock is a type of stock which forms the majority of ownership in every company. Common stock shares are proof of ownership within an organization. Common stock holders elect directors of the company and participate with the profits of the business through dividends. In the event that the company goes into bankruptcy and liquidates, senior or secured lenders get paid first. They are then unsecured, or junior lenders, and then preferred stockholders then the common stockholders.

Another form of finance that businesses could issue as an alternative to their ordinary stock is called preferred stock.

Preferred Stock is a type of stock which provides special treatment for dividends. Preferred dividends is akin to the interest earned on loans. Stockholders who are preferred stockholders receive dividends prior to common stockholders get dividends. The dividends may be given in shares instead of cash.

The common as well as preferred stocks are divided into two types par value and additional Paidin Capital, or APIC. Most of the cash is credited to APIC.

The account for Par Value an unofficial value of one cent, and is a method to track the outstanding shares. Par value refers to an amount of money that is attributed to every share. It's an undetermined number that is usually $.01. If a company had more than 1,000 shares, there would be $100.00 on the account for par value. Par Value could even be $0.001. Par Value does not have any connection with the market value of the stock. Consider it an investment.

This account, also known as the Additional Paid in Capital (APIC) account is the place where the value that is paid to purchase a shares of common stock, less par value is reported. If a common stock with an amount of $0.01 is purchased at a price of $15, the account Common Stock will be credited with $0.01 and the associated account called the Additional Paidin Capital (APIC) or APIC Account will get paid to $14.99 (and cash is debited at $15.00). Retained Earnings are the equity account for stockholders that tracks and records the income earned by an organization from the time of its creation up to the date of its balance sheet in addition to dividends that were declared between when it was founded until the date on its balance sheet. The account records the earnings or losses accrued since a firm was founded. These profits and losses go on behalf of shareholders. When the year is over, year, the amount of profit or loss reported in the income statement will be used to alter the amount of money in this account. To make a comparison to your life experience Think of your the Retained Earnings account as a money left after you've paid the expenses.

Contra Accounts

A contra account is used to offset the balance on a associated account to that account. If the associated account is a asset account the contra asset account is utilized for offsets using the balance of a credit. If the account that is linked to it is an equity or liability account and a contra equity or a liability account is utilized for offset using an account with a debit balance. Equity accounts for stockholders typically contain credits.

Contra equity accounts fall under one of the categories of equity accounts which have balances of debit. The debit balance of an equity account of the owner is in opposition (contra) to the equity account's normal credit balance. One example of a contra equity account for stockholders is Treasury Stock. Treasury stock is the corporation's own stock which was bought from stockholders and is kept by the corporate. As it's an outstanding stock, and not held in the possession by shareholders. It is required to be weighed against the value of the shareholder's shares to determine the proper value of the capital. This is why you need the contra account. Depreciation is a counter account that decreases the worth of assets similarly.

Now we have discussed the main equity accounts in accounts. Certain accounts may have different names but they all have identical purposes. The equity section for stockholders on a balance sheet is as follows:

Stockholder's Equity

Capital that is paid in

Common Stock

Preferred Stock

Additional Paidin Capital Common Stock

Additional Paidin Capital Preferred Stock

Additional Paidin Capital Treasury Stock

Retained Earnings

Less: Treasury Stock

Total Stockholder's Equity

A Cash Flow Statement (the other financial statement)

Alongside the Income Statement as well as the Balance Sheet there's an additional financial statement, the Cash Flow Statement. It is the Cash Flow Statement is a reconciliation of the income Statement to the financial position of the company (the balance of the account at the banks) through the addition and subtraction of revenue and expenditures that are properly reflected within the income Statement and Balance Sheet, however they aren't cash instances. The depreciation process and the changes to Account Receivables are an example of noncash transactions. The reconciled balance of the bank account is the amount that will be used to create the cash account located that is at the top of the column for assets in the balance sheet. This is vital. It is the way that financial statements work together.

The requirement for a Cash flow statement is due to Accrual Accounting in which we record things like Payables and

Receivables and depreciation, in order to give a better overview of the activities of an organization by comparing the expenses and revenues. The "noncash" transactions distort the Income Statement in relation to the amount of cash that actually was deposited and taken out of the business and also the amount that is at the account at the bank. The Operation portion of the Cash Statement, also known as the Flow Statement is able to reconcile these disparities.

In addition to Operation in addition, there are two more aspects that make up the Cash Flow Statement, which are a part of the Operations section that are Investing and Financing. The Investing section reveals the amount of money used to purchase capital equipment which aren't reported as an expense on the Income Statement as they were capitalized as assets.

Chapter 3: Sample Cash Flow Statement

On this page, you get an example of straightforward Cash Flow statement. Because they differ in content and format, it's recommended to have an instant look at some examples. Google the phrase "Cash Flow Statement" and you'll find a lot of different types of formats and presentation.

Statement of Cash Flows

For the Year Ended December 31, 2018

(In Millions of Dollars)

Operating Activities

Net Income from Operations: $10,000

Add: Depreciation Expense 100

Total Operating Activities $10,100

Investing Activities

Purchase of Equipment (1,000)

Sale of Equipment 500

Total Investing Activities (500)

Financing Activities

Increase in Long Term Debt $2,500

Issuance of Stock 5,000

Dividends Paid (3,000)

Total Financing Activities $4,500

Net Change in Cash Flow $14,100

Financial Statement Interconnections and Flow

All three Financial Statements are interconnected and they flow together. In essence, you begin a year with a balance sheet that displays the financial situation at the start of the year. Then there is the Income Statement which outlines what was done during the period. Finally, you get it is a Balance Sheet at the close each year. The Cash Flow Statement reconciles the position of cash starting with the number Net Income in the lower part of your Income Statement. The number of cash calculated from the Cash Flow statement is in addition to the cash on the Balance Sheet. This amount must be in line with the cash actually in the bank. It is then calculated as the cash account balance in the upper left (Asset column) on the final Year (EOY) balance sheet. The number for Net Income from the Income Statement then gets placed in the Retained Earnings amount within the equity section (left right hand section) on the last page of the Year (EOY) balance sheet. If it is done properly then all numbers will be in line and the assets will be the same as the liabilities and Equity in the End of Year Balance Sheet.

Consider it the system that has two Balance Sheets that act as bookends of an

Income Statement. The Cash Flow Statement is utilized to compare the Net Income (or loss) in the lower part of an Income Statement to the actual amount of cash stored in the account. This method records each dollar that's entered and out of an organization during the time. Knowing the three statements of financials can help you evaluate the viability, financial health and potential of any business and take logical informed investment decisions.

Although it is a short section is a bridge between the functions of financial statements. It could be the "aha" moment for you. This was my experience when I realised how it all worked in harmony. The conceptual idea of accounting will give you the context that will keep your mind from becoming lost within the nuances.

The Role of Auditors

In accordance with the SEC guidelines and rules for being legally able to trade at a stock exchange public company's financials are to be prepared by the business before being reviewed and audited by an external Certified Public Accountant (CPA).

Private companies with a lot of investors are also required to have audited financial statements in order to make sure that the accounting methods and financial statements are prepared with integrity and transparency.

What exactly is an auditor?

Auditing involves reviewing the financial statements that are prepared and written by the business to ensure they are in conformity to GAAP as well as other regulations. Auditors also "test" the numbers by asking for and reviewing the supporting documentation like invoices, cheques as well as bills and contracts. They also send letters to companies' banks to verify bank balances, and also contact the lawyers that they have collaborated with to verify there aren't any unresolved liabilities or lawsuits which haven't been made public.

The Auditing Process

Within any business, there are many opportunities to commit fraud. Managers of companies are entrusted with the potential to profit from finances for personal gains. In public companies, the annual audit is legally required and the shareholders of numerous privately held firms, such as bankers, are also required to submit annual accounts that are audited.

Audits are designed to safeguard against the misrepresentation of financial details to boost outcomes, reduce tax burdens as well as concealing fraud. avoid reporting latent liability. Audits are the process of collecting information on the systems of finance and documents pertaining to the financials of a business.

Audits of financials are conducted to determine the accuracy and integrity of accounting practices and data in addition for a review of internal control systems of the organization. Audits are performed by an independent third party accounting group which is led by a certified accountant who has been recognized as CPA. CPA.

For work in other businesses' finances, you need to be an CPA. The United States a CPA will be a graduate of the Uniform Certified Public Accountant Examination, and will have met other educational and work experience requirements of the state for membership with their accounting profession's statespecific organization. There is no requirement to have the qualifications of CPA to be a CPA to be employed by internal companies as an employee, either in financial or accounting.

Because the auditor can't have all the information about an organization Audits are designed to give reasonable assurance in the knowledge that statements do not suffer of any material error. Testing and sampling of records is carried out during audits in order to determine statistically the probability that accounting was correctly performed by the business. The financial statements is considered to be "true and fair" once they have been deemed to be without material mistakes. Auditors confirm this with their opinion statement that is presented prior to the financials of the final presented presentation. The final opinion on financial statements is based on audit evidence gathered. It is found in the first paragraph of the audited financial statement.

GAAP and IFSR

GAAP stands for General accepted Accounting Principles. They are the accounting rules and accounting practices which have been accepted by accounting professionals within the United States. In the rest of the world, accounting has adopted a new standard known as IFSR. IFSR refers to International Financial Reporting Standards. This is the accounting standard utilized in over 110 countries but it is not used within the United States. Both standards aim to record the economic impact in accounting as precisely and clear as it is possible.

There exist two distinct accounting systems in the world leads to complexities which pose a challenge for those who use accounting data and an issue for multinational companies. International businesses must maintain two financial records and submit two set of financial statements that are audited. This is costly and timeconsuming of additional work. Even though there's been attempts to integrate the two standards into a single global standards, they haven't reached a consensus on one.

Summary

Users of Accounting Information

Managers must know how their entire company is faring or how their department is performing. Managers might require to get feedback ASAP regarding how a brand current marketing campaign or pricing strategy is performing. How and when accounting for transactions is vital to the users of accounting data. Customers require timely information about how their business is performing for them to take the right decisions.

In addition to the interests of the management, there are other external customers of accounting data like:

Bankers that are looking to assess your credit worthiness as well as the ability to repay loans

Vendors keen on your capacity to pay, and also your credit worthiness,

Investors that want to determine whether they should invest, or how their investment is doing,

Stock Analysts, who study businesses and make a decision on whether they're an investment for their clients,

Potential clients, particularly with largeticket goods or services. are looking to ensure that the firm is reliable and can assist and provide spare parts.

Taxing authorities are interested in knowing how much revenue the company has earned or made or.

The reporting of the business's results activities using an accrual system is essential to the parties who are concerned about the health and performance of the business. Accrual offers a far more precise picture of business's operations for those not involved in everyday operations, but who need to be aware of the details that affect operations.

The method by which this report of accounting data is organized, prepared and presented is via Financial Statements.

Chapter 4: Financial Statement Analysis

Accounting and Finance have a lot in common. The starting point in Corporate Finance is to comprehend and read Financial Statements. Analysis of the financial statements, and then of projections and assumptions based on this analysis is the following process. Analysis of financial statements is the process of looking at the company's financial statements, and comparing their analysis with sectors and businesses for better investment and operating decisions. The method of analysis involves particular techniques to evaluate the risk and efficiency, financial health and the potential future of a company. It is possible to analyze the performance of a specific business over the course of time, such as annual results. This is known as Horizontal Analysis. We can analyze different performance indicators in a short time. This is known as Vertical Analysis. It is possible to create metrics for different industries to provide an average to measure our organization to. This is referred to as benchmarking. It is also possible to aggregate diverse industry segments and observe what they do in comparison to one another. This kind of analysis may aid in determining the best place you should allocate your investment dollars within an investment portfolio. Additionally, it can be used to assess how a the management team performs in relation to other teams.

Financial statements are analysed and reviewed by a wide range of stakeholder groups, such as equity and debt investors, taxing agencies, and government agencies. authorities as well as management decision makers. That is exactly what experts in the field of credit do. They have different stakeholder interests and use a number of strategies to meet their requirements. Some capitalists are concerned in the potential longterm growth of their company, or perhaps the longevity and expansion of dividends. A few equity investors such as hedge funds might be searching for hidden risks and potential pitfalls to profit from the shortterm potential of a position. They are searching for companies that could be in the process of collapse. They want to make sure that the principal and interest on the company's debt securities is paid on time and on time. Commercial lenders and banks employ financial statement analysis in their credit evaluation to determine the appropriateness of loans or lend. Rating agencies such as Moody's, Standard and Poors as well as Fitch do financial statements analysis to determine the creditworthiness and risk of a company and its credit. Managers utilize it to assess how their companies are performing in relation to its historical results, its goals, and the industry they operate in.

Financial statement analysis techniques comprise fundamental analysis, the utilization of financial ratios, and DuPont analysis. Analytical methods can be performed either vertically or horizontally manner across the company.

For estimating future results, the historical data can be used in conjunction with the assumptions concerning the prospects of the business and its future economic climate. Profits that will be earned in the future is utilized to estimate the value of an enterprise. It is the basic idea behind Business Valuation as well as Corporate Finance.

Before getting to the details of these methods, we'll first look at a history of the way in which financial statement analysis came into existence and evolved.

History of Financial Statement Analysis

The crash of the stock market on October 29, 1929, was a traumatic event which resulted in the Great Depression and worldwide economic conflict. The crash also triggered tensions in the political and social spheres. The events raised questions about the legitimacy of Capitalism and Democracy as unsettling problems with the system were discovered and a lot of people felt the effects.

One of the main reasons for this issue was the fact that a lot of companies which traded on the market didn't provide any meaningful data about the status of their operations. No financial statements were available to look over. No transparency was provided. To clean up the mess and ensure trust in the investors of the stock market, Roosevelt administration established the Securities and Exchange Commission (SEC) to supervise and regulate the markets for stocks. Roosevelt required a person to lead the SEC that was knowledgeable of all the tricks and pitfalls of the market, so that they could identify and fight fraud.. The person who stepped up to this challenge is Joseph P. Kennedy. Joe was the future President John F. Kennedy's father, and was known stock manipulation expert and patriot.

One of the new SEC guidelines was that every business had to file financial statements compiled by an external thirdparty auditor under a strict system of accounting guidelines known as GAAP, which stands for Generally Accepted Accounting Principles. The financial statements, along with details about operations were required to be submitted and released to the public by the SEC annually. This document is known as an 10K. This type of information, along with transparency allows investors and the general public to gain an understanding of the business's activities and potential and decide how much or not to invest.

The regulations seem intuitive and sensible today yet it was strong and striking, and an absolute revelation in the moment. Fundamental analysis, which was a method for analyzing the new data was a hit quickly. Today the 10K remains the primary document, and the fundamental analysis is a instrument used for the analysis of stock markets and for corporate investment decisions.

Fundamental Analysis

The SEC as well as the regulations for financial reporting was enacted by two statutes The '33 Act as well as the 34 Act. Benjamin Graham and David Dodd released their groundbreaking publication "Security Analysis" in 1934. Warren Buffett is a wellknown fan of Graham as well as Dodd's philosophy.

It is the Graham and Dodd approach is called Fundamental Analysis and includes: Analyzing the economics of industry as well as Company analysis. Company analysis is the most important area of analysis for financial statements. Based on these three types of analyses, the value of the security is calculated. Fundamental analysis is the way analysts, bankers and investors make their longterm investment choices.

The book has been through numerous revisions and edits, and is now available in an updated version. It is worth checking the book out, especially should you ever want to emulate Warren. Another person who supports Graham as well as Dodd are Bill Ackman the American hedge fund manager. Bill is the cofounder and the CEO of Pershing Square Capital Management. Bill is also a billionaire.

Horizontal and Vertical Analysis

Horizontal analysis is a way of comparing financial information across time, typically using financial statements that have been in the past like the income statement. If we compare this information with the previous one, we are looking for differences in certain line items, such as more or less revenue from sales, earnings or specific expenditures. Horizontal analysis can be used to identify patterns that can be extrapolated to determine the future's performance. However, remember that the past's performance may not be an accurate predictor of the future's performance.

Vertical analysis is a ratio analysis that is performed using financial statements. It's a the ratio analysis. Items of interest on the financial statements are shown as a percentage of a different line item. In the example above, on an income statement, every line item is listed as a percentage of sales.

Financial Ratios

Financial ratios are a potent tool that help assess the company's upside risks, risk, and downside. There are four major types of ratios namely liquidity ratios the ratio of profitability, activity ratios, and leverage ratios. They're typically studied with respect to time and against competitors within the same industry. Utilizing these ratios "normalizes" the numbers so you are able to evaluate companies using applestoapples comparisons.

Liquidity and Solvency

Both liquidity and solvency related to the company's viability and financial health. Solvency is the term used to describe an organization's capability to pay its financial obligations over the long term. Liquidity is the capacity to meet shortterm obligations. It is also an indicator of the speed with which assets can be sold in order to generate funds.

Solvency is a company which owns more than what the amount it has to pay. It is a company with a positive net worth, and has an acceptable amount of debt. An organization with sufficient liquid funds may have sufficient cash in its bank account to cover the bills and still in danger of financial ruin in the future. If a business has met the requirements for liquidity by being not insolvent. The healthy companies are solvent and have sufficient liquidity.

The ratio of liquidity is used to assess whether a business is able to cover its expenses and satisfy its obligations in the near future (current obligations). Solvency ratios measure of the speed at which a business will convert its assets to cash in the event of financial problems or is in danger of being threatened by bankruptcy. They both measure various factors of whether and how long the company is able to pay its expenses and stay operating.

The current ratio as well as the quick ratio comprise both common ratios of liquidity. The current ratio represents current assets/current liabilities. It determines the amount of liquid (cash) can be used for current obligations (bills or other obligation). Quick ratio = (current assets + inventories) (current liabilities inventories). This measure an organization's capacity to meet the shortterm commitments it has made based on the assets that are most liquid that is, therefore, it does not include inventories as part of its assets. This is sometimes referred to as"acidtest ratio. "acidtest ratio."

Solvency ratios are used to assess the capacity of an organization to fulfill its obligations over the long term. It is usually utilized by bankers and lenders. The ratio relates cash flows with obligations. Calculating the solvency ratio involves these actions:

The total of all noncash costs is included in aftertax net income. It is a rough estimate of the money flowing through the company. It is possible to find the figures to calculate in the Operation section in the Cash Flow statement.

Take all the shortterm and longerterm obligations. This is called the Total Liabilities in the balance sheet. Divide the cash flow by the total liabilities.

The formula to calculate the ratio is:

(Net aftertax income + Noncash expenses)/(Shortterm liabilities + Longterm liabilities)

Higher percentages indicate an increase in the capacity to cover the obligations of a company for the longer term.

Keep in mind that any estimates made for an extended period of time are typically incorrect. Many factors influence the capability to be paid over the longterm. The use of any ratio for estimating solvency must be treated with caution. salt.

The ratio of profitability

Ratios of profitability help determine how successful a business is. For a company to become profitable, the company must cover its costs. Breakeven points and gross profit ratio tackle the issue of cost coverage by addressing it in various ways. The breakeven point determines the amount of cash that a business will need to raise in order to be able to keep up in operating expenses. Gross profit ratio is equivalent to (revenue the price of the goods sold)/revenue. The ratio gives a brief picture of revenue expected that could be used to calculate operating costs and overheads of operation.

Other examples of profit ratios are the profit margin or return on assets as well as returns on equity. The more valuable these ratios is, the more profitable a business is. The higher the value in relation to the ratio of a competitor or a similar ratio that was in a prior period suggests that the company has been performing fairly good and moving towards the proper direction.

Return on Equity

Return on Equity (ROE) = Net Income / Average Shareholders' Equity

Earnings per Share

Earnings per Share (EPS) is the percentage of the profit earned by the business that is allotted to every remaining share of common stock.

Earnings per share can be an extremely reliable gauge of the efficiency of an organization. it's one of the most frequently used indicators of profit.

Ratios of activity

The activity ratios can be calculated to determine how the management is managing the resources of the business. The activity ratios are a measure of sales against other assets accounts. The most commonly used assets used include inventory, accounts receivable and the total assets. Because most businesses are characterized by a large amount of assets that are tied to accounts receivable, inventory, and working capital they are utilized as the basis of the most commonly used activities ratios.

The term "Accounts Receivable" (AR) can be defined as the amount owed to a company in exchange to purchase products or services via a credit account. The amount of time that passes before AR can be collected is vital due to the fact that anticipated revenue needs to be funded in some manner. The turnover of accounts receivables shows how quickly a company is able to collect the amount owed and also indicates the amount of cash available to the receivables.

Accounts Receivable Turnover = Total Credit Sales/Average Accounts Receivable

The typical collection time in days equals 360 days multiplied by turnover of accounts receivable. Another ratio provides an understanding of AR collection.

Average Collection Period = 365 Days/Accounts Receivable Turnover

Analysts often utilize the median collection period to assess the efficiency of a business's capability to get payments from customers with credit. The period of collection is not longer than the terms of credit the company offers to its clients.

An important indicator of profit is the capability to manage the inventory. The inventory is the money and investments that don't generate a profit until the item is eventually sold. The longer an inventory is kept more, the less profitmaking an organization could become. A greater ratio of turnover suggests more interest in goods as well as better cash management, and as a result, a lower probability of stock becoming obsolete. The most accurate measurement of how much inventory is the percentage of turnover in inventory. It is determined as the annual total sales or cost of the goods sold (COGS) multiplied by the price of inventory.

Inventory Turnover = Total Annual Sales or Cost of Goods Sold/Average Inventory

The use of the price of products which are sold within the numerator may give a better indication of turnover on inventory since it permits a clear comparability with other companies. The different businesses have their own prices for their goods which can make it difficult to do an the applestoapples comparability.

The inventory cost average is often used in the denominator in order to account for seasonal variances.

Leverage ratios

Leverage ratios are a measure of the extent of a business's use of credit to finance its activities as well as its assets. The ratio between equity and debt is one of the most commonly used. It is calculated using:

(Longterm debt and shortterm debt + leases)+ Equity

Businesses with a high ratio of debt require steady and predictable income streams for the purpose of servicing the debt. companies whose earnings fluctuate and have less predictability should depend more heavily on equity for the capital structure. The leverage also has implications on liquidity.

Startups depend almost exclusively on Equity since they don't have sources of income or income which can be used to service the debt.

DuPont analysis

DuPont analysis was invented in the DuPont Corporation in the 1920s as a method to analyze the investments they made across different businesses and activities. Being a conglomerate in its early days it needed a method to evaluate the performances of various businesses so that they can make better choices about how and where to invest their funds. It is now popular as a tool for management and investment instrument.

What is the driver behind ROE?

DuPont Analysis analyzes Return on Equity through deconstructing its primary drivers.

DuPont Analysis is an expression that breaks down the return of equity (ROE) into three components.

The fundamental formula is:

ROE (Profit margin) = (Profit margin)*(Asset turnover)*(Equity multiplyer) =

(Net Income/Sales)*(Sales/Assets)*(Assets/Equity) = (Net Income/Equity)

The three components are:

Efficacy: determined by the profit margin

Operating efficiency is calculated by turnover of the asset

Financial leverage is determined by the an equity multiplier

DuPont analysis allows you to identify the cause of a higher (or lower) performance by looking at firms in similar industries or even between different industries. Additionally, it provides a greater depth of knowledge by breaking away the most important factors and variables that drive ROE. Equity. In addition, ROE is certainly one of the metrics which stock investor (stock investors) are keen on.

Chapter 5: Managing Working Capital

Working Capital

Working Capital is a term that refers to the quantity of cash and liquid assets that are available to run in a company. It's a financial measure that measures operational liquidity. Working capital represents the gap between the current assets and current liabilities. In addition to fixed assets such as equipment and plants Working capital is considered as a component of the operating capital. Management of working capital is managing inventories and accounts payable, as well as accounts receivable payable, as well as cash.

Current assets and liabilities also include three financial accounts particularly important. These accounts are the ones of business in which managers have the biggest immediate influence and impact:

Receivables (current capital)

Inventory (current assets) and

Accounts payable (current liability)

The shortterm loan and the current part of longerterm loan (payable in 12 month intervals) are essential since they're temporary claims against current assets that are usually secured by assets of a long term nature. Lines of credit are popular types of debt that are shortterm in nature.

The increase in net working capital suggests that the company either accrued more assets in the current period or diminished existing obligations. The financing and management of working capital is an important operation challenge, specifically when a company is rapidly expanding.

Managing Working Capital

Receivables and inventory can be funded with a line of credit (revolving loan, like the credit card). Management of receivables makes certain that your clients make payments and pay on time and you must have cash is in your doors! The ratio of accounts Receivables are characterized by their turnover. It is a percentage mentioned earlier, which indicates how quickly credit sales are that are received.

Controlling inventories is a way of to avoid allowing inventories to build up. This is accomplished by keeping track of production activity, sales and also the inventory turnover ratio. It is important to have enough inventory so that you are able to handle a surge in sales. But you shouldn't be in danger of having too many stock that isn't able to be removed. This is particularly important for products with a brief time frame and are likely to be deemed outdated. If they are not promptly sold this could lead to you having to drastically reduce prices on products so that they can be sold. It could result in losses. Operations Management is a discipline specifically focused on this issue as well as preventing potential issues.

It is easy to determine the performance of a business with regard to this by looking over the balance sheet of their business and compare the current Assets with Current Liabilities as well as examining if there's an increase in the amount of current Assets. Check this for the past few years, and see whether there has been a shift of Working Capital and if it results from a rise of inventory.

The Time Value of Money

"The importance of money flows from it being a link between the present and the future".

John Maynard Keynes.

Keynes was a genius who had a deep understanding of the economics and financial markets. His insights weren't only academic or intellectual. He was able to make two billions of dollars: one on the market for stocks and another within the art industry. He was a savvy investor and placed his money where his mouth was.

The key monetary element that connects the past and the future are the interest rate or discount rate. If you've got a current value that you wish to estimate a future value this is known as"an interest rate. If you've got future values that you wish to determine their value today, then we employ the term discount rate. Discount rates and interest rates are both aspects of one coin. To use the metaphor of money.

Days of Future Past

Two sets of data we utilize for corporate finance both prospective and retrospective. The retrospective data are compiled into financial statements. They are the performance history of an organization and are able to be analysed, compared and then extrapolated. Ratios are an instrument of financial statement analysis, and we have just talked about them.

Data on prospective prospects is included into financial projections. These are the management's projections of how the company will be performing in the near future. The projections are analyzed as well as riskadjusted, and the present value of these projected cash flows could be estimated. This article will discuss the aspects of finance that are forwardlooking using the notion of price of time (TVM).

The time is the currency, literally. If you are in the position of earning a certain amount and you are able to receive it sooner, the earlier you get it, the higher the value. Interest rates define this relation between the present value and the the future value. It is the most fundamental idea of finance. This is the connection between future and present value through a variety of angles. I'll explain the concept in various ways so that you can let the concept sink in.

TVM provides the theoretical basis of finance. This is the fundamental basis of the way banks operate as well as how bonds and stocks are priced, the way businesses and assets are evaluated and how they are evaluated and evaluated, and the way you be thinking about the origins and purpose of the concept of money.

One bird in the hands is worth a pair on the rock.

Today's money is worth greater than receiving the exact amount in the near future, as well, the worth of the possibility of receiving money decreases as you move further into the future it is promised to pay. The pace in which the value of one's dollar in the near future diminishes in comparison to what it is today in direct proportion to the amount of a dollar that is invested currently will rise over time. It is important to take a moment to let the concept take in. The present and the future value are the two different sides of the same coin (pun intended!) and are connected to one another by the rate of interest.

The idea of price of the time can explain how interest can be made or earned. The interest, regardless of whether it's in a bank loan or loan, compensates the depositor or lender for the period of value of the cash. The risk is related to the uncertainty of repaying and interest rates are a reflection of the amount of uncertain or the risk. One of the main reasons why credit card companies have such steep rate of interest is the chance of another person who default on their debts is built into the interest rate.

TVM can also be a key element in investing. Investment is all about managing risk and returning. A person who invests is prepared to save funds now, if they anticipate positive returns on investing in the near future. The expected return is correlated to the likelihood of recouping one's investment in the near future. The greater the risk that is perceived is, the greater the expected amount of return. A person is ready to sell their capital if greed is greater than fears, when the expectation of yield is greater than the risk that they are assuming.

Discounting Cash Flows

The main focus part of finance for corporations is to calculate the current value of coming cash flows. The concept of this is founded on the value of time for cash. An organization is basically an organization that produces annual cash flows to the foreseeable future. The challenge is to determine these future cash flows, and the extent to which they could expand or shrink, and the risk in achieving them.

That's where you'll need the ability to refine your crystal ball and perform a deep examination of your business, its market and competition. The information you gather is put into a spreadsheet that contains financial projections. The bottom line shows the expected cash flow for each year. The cash flows are discounted to their present value using an amount that is a discount. This is based on what comparable investment options, which are simply flowing streams of anticipated cash flows that are priced on the market as well as the risks that are that are specific to the specific company or asset that we're considering purchasing or selling.

It is the fundamental concept of valuation. It is a way of estimating the value of something. The value of something can be determined in auctions where bidders compete and the bidder with the most money is the winner. How do bidders decide the amount they can bid, and what is considered excessive?

The stock market is basically an auction in which investors put bids, which are the amount they're willing to pay to purchase a share as well as asking what amount an investor would be willing to trade for. Businesses, assets, even startups that do not have revenue yet are evaluated by this method.

The method of calculating the actual value of cash flows is essential for valuing startups with no history of revenue as well as assets firms who are projected to grow fast. When this happens, you cannot count on past performance and past performance to determine an estimate based on the current assets or P/E.

It is the method that is favored by the investment bankers and venture capitalists. It is also used by hedge funds, private equity as well as savvy investors as well as credit analysts as well as CFOs. It's simple to comprehend and you'll be amazed at how efficient and effective it is.

Present Value and Future Value

100 dollars invested over a year, which earns interest of 5%, will become $105 at the end of one year. Therefore 100 dollars paid today or $105 that is paid 1 year from now will be worth the same amount for a

person who is expecting an annual return of 5. So, a $100 investment in one year, earning an interest rate of 5% has an estimated value of $105 in the future. It is assumed that inflation will be at 0.

The formula in this scenario could be as follows:

$105 = $100 (1+.05)

The most common formula to solve the future value problem is

FV = PV (1+r)

Where

Future value is the FV

PV is the value of present PV is the present value

R is the rate of interest

The reciprocal formula for solving for the present value is a juggle of elements using algebraic basics and then recasts the equation in the following manner:

$PV = FV/(1+r)$

This simply places it on the (1+r) term in the opposite side of the equation in order to find a solution PV. This is done by subdividing both sides (1+r). If you find this confusing, simply substitute (1+r) with"X" for now.

$FV = PV\ X$

If you split each side by X, then you'll get:

$FV/X = PV\ X/X$

Because the expression X/X is equivalent to 1 The term disappears from that part of the equation. This leaves us with

$FV/X = PV$

Replace the X by (1+r) and you'll see how our equation is derived.

It is important to make sure that you fully understand this as it's the foundation of the valuation of assets. It is the method used to estimate the cash flows in the future by calculating their present value.

The concept can be used to determine the present value of an anticipated income stream that will be generated for the coming years. In this instance, the each year's cash flow is discounted, and the results are then summed up which is then an estimate of the value at present for all income streams.

Here is a link to the beginning of a series in Khan Academy on the time value of money and present value calculations http://bit.ly/1Ul43VT Sal Khan is great at explaining concepts and these videos will be very helpful in solidifying your understanding of this concept.

Net Present Value

A financial instrument that embodies concepts of the connection between future and present values of cash is known as NPV Net Present Value. When you finish this article, you'll know the way it functions and what you can do with it. Five minutes in the future will change your lifestyle.

Net Present Value (NPV) is the standard method of analysis utilized in financial analysis and making investment decisions. Excel spreadsheets such as Excel simplify it to utilize. We will discuss the definition of NPV can mean, and how it's determined, and what you can do you can use it.

NPV is the term which binds it all when it comes to understanding the financials of corporations. NPV is the foundation of financial understanding.

We invest our money in initiatives that will earn money in the near future. Pay now, and plan to reap the benefits later on. Most often, a asset or project is able to generate streams of revenue as well as profits over the course of time. There is also an asset whose primary purpose is to save money.

The ability to figure out if the money flow that is coming in the future will be worth more than amount we have to put into in it to purchase or construct it. The tool we use is NPV. utilize to do this analysis.

The method we use to make how to decide whether we should fund an initiative or determine the worth of an asset is by turning this stream of dollars from the future to current dollars.

After that, we evaluate the total of the present value with costs; if cost is greater than the value of the present that we won't make the deal. However, if there is less than that then it's considered to be to be a bargain.

This is how the projects are evaluated in terms of whether they are a go or not and also how revenuegenerating asset and acquisitions are assessed to be sold, purchased and merger.

In our previous blog posts we examined and calculated worth of cash flows that are expected to come in the future before bringing them back down in value. Net Present Value (NPV) expands on this notion one step further, and also takes into account the transactional aspects.

We have to "purchase" the future cash flow by either:

You can purchase a bond or stocks, or

Buying a business (or

Purchase an asset that generates income (or

Taking on a project that involves creating or constructing the incomeproducing asset.

Net Present Value "nets out" the cost to acquire futuristic cash flow. NPV evaluates the value in current dollars with the current value of anticipated earnings or benefits, also in dollars of today. It is worthwhile if the cost is lower than the value of future benefit.

NPV is the primary instrument used to evaluate assets, and to make decisions regarding acquisitions, projects, mergers or acquisitions. These spreadsheets are quite complex when they're filled with all costs as well as revenue and expense projections along with assumptions on the timing of events and risks, however the principle is to assess the value of costs against future gains and then evaluate them applestoapples when considering the cost of time.

NPV provides a straightforward answer: is the present worth of the entire amount that will be received over the course of the venture outweigh the much we need to put aside to get it? Net present value means an expression of the net difference between these two streams of money: the money that is going out as well as the cash that is coming in.

It is important to know if it is more than zero. If it's higher than zero Then the expenses are lower than the rewards so we must either complete this project or invest an investment.

The deciding factor is if NPV is greater than zero or lower than. It is possible to construct the formula to calculate NPV following the exact same formula as we discussed in our previous blog post about discounting cash flows. The gold standard is NPV, but when used in conjunction with IRR can lead to more effective analysis and decisionmaking. I will discuss the IRR (internal rate of return) in a subsequent blog article.

NPV is the value that's being received from the project, in terms of cash flows less the cost of initialization.

The formula can be described to be the first cost with a minus symbol before it. with cash flow for period 1 discounted for one time back, and the cash flow during period 2 which was discounted by two times back, and the cash flow during period 3 discounted for three times You get the picture and all other cash flows being discounted by the time of their arrival.

What we're doing is taking the original cost, and then weighing it against the current value of money coming into. Then, we "net" the two numbers. A minus symbol is displayed for the expenses, and plus sign on each of the actual values of cash flows. The focus is on how the total amount of money flowing out is compared to the cash coming in.

Imagine it as an equilibrium. If we have the information about the initial amount of investment as well as the flow of cash coming into the project in the near future We can calculate the NPV by the sum of the two streams; it is the difference between these two streams.

The initial investment grows greater and the NPV shrinks. The NPV is greater than zero or lower than 0 is contingent upon the ratio between funds going out and funds entering. Let's solve a puzzle and calculate an NPV using the real world.

Review the flow of cash flows and determine the NPV, assuming that the discount rate is 15%.

EXAMPLE PROJECT

Today

Year: 0 1 2 Sum (NPV)

$3,000 $1,500 $1800 $300

We should consider whether it's worthwhile to undertake this task. Today, in period zero it is necessary to pay $3,000 to be able to access the cash flow in the future. Would it be worth it put aside that money? What can we hope to receive from it?

How much cash is from the project? The project has one cash flow of $1500 arriving at the close of the first year. We also have an additional cash flow of $1800 that will be in the final days of year 2. If we simply add the cash flows, less than 3000 (it is not minus since it's a cost) plus 1500 and 1800, we'll get a figure of $300. The company is making money. In this regard, it's profitable. In fact, the money flowing into is more than that which is being withdrawn.

This is the total of all cash flows and that's with no discount. It's not accounted for the fact that we'll have waiting a year before we obtain the $1,500 amount, and wait for a second year to receive the $1,800. Keep in mind that to make use of money, you need to be able to pay for it. There is an expense for capital. The question is, what are we required to cover? In this scenario it is this discount rate of 15. This is the price of capital in this case.

Today

Year: 0 1 2 Sum (NPV)

$3,000 $1,500 $1800 $300

Present

Value: $1500/(1.15)^1$ $1800/(1.15)^2$

NPV

@15% $3,000 + $1,304.35 + $1,361.06 = $334.59

Then we need to alter our cash flow to reflect the value of time by reducing them to their current value. Take $1,500, and discount it by one time at 15%, and we end up with $1,304.35. We then take $1,800 and reduce it by two times at 15%. We come up with $1,361.06. When we add the current value of the cash flows, the result is the sum of $334.59 This indicates that the plan is destroying value. The project is not worthwhile.

It's a viable project however, we're not going to take it on. How could we not desire to work on a project which makes money? All it boils down to is 15% discount rate. This 15% is what is the threshold rate to determine the viability of the venture. The project could be profitable however it's not financially viable enough to justify the 15% required return. If our bosses, we or investors demand the return of 15% in order in order to cover the cost of the project, we're likely to give it to them on the same project.

We will look at some of the major drivers in this Net present value calculations. The first is the cash flow. Naturally, having more cash is superior to lesser. Another factor is timing. The more cash flow is into the near future, the more it is discounted.

The third factor could be a discount rate. The more discount rates are high more cash flows are discounted, and also the more expensive the NEV. Lower discount rates more discounting it will be greater the benefit of the project. Lower discount rates, higher NPV. Higher discount rates, lower NPV

Net present value is a measure of benchmarking. It's the most efficient instrument for capital budgeting. It includes the time of cash flow, and also considers the potential cost since the discount rate determines the essence of what other possibilities we could have using the cash.

Discounting implicitly includes the cost of opportunity. It also includes the risk. If we feel that the project has a higher risk then what do we do? It is possible to increase the discount rate so that it reflects the higher danger.

Chapter 6: Financial Literacy Glossary Of Terms

They are key concepts and words, presented ordered alphabetically, that are related with Financial Literacy. Utilize this tool when you are navigating your way to becoming acquainted with the terms used.

Accounting

Accounting is the process of recording and report of financial transactions within an organization. It involves documentation of the genesis of a deal, such as a sale or receipt of a bill via the postal mail. It also includes its acknowledgment in the ledger book as well as its processing to process the money transfer or a deposit to the bank, as well as the report and summation in accounting statements. These financial statements are essential to the operation of a business in paying taxes as well as making investment and operating decision.

Accounts Payable

Accounts Payable is a type of liability that represents the amount due to an individual creditor. For most businesses, checks are made in batches, and the obligations will be entered into accounts for Accounts Payable before they're paid. The account is typically a present account that is shown in the Balance Sheet. The term "Accounts Payable" refers to the amount that the company is owed for the delivery of services or goods offered. Accounts Payable are accounts connected to the Accrual accounting method.

Accounts Receivable

Account Receivable refers to an amount that is owed to an organization following a successful sales transaction or services performed. It is an asset that is related to revenue from sales. It is a present asset.

The Accounts Receivalbe account is that is part of the Accrual accounting method.

Accrual Basis

Accrual basis is a type of accounting in which revenue is recognized as it is earned and not the moment when funds are actually earned and when expenses are they are incurred, rather than when the money is payed. This is the process to recognize revenue when goods are purchased, sold or given or delivered, as well as when services are provided. The recognition of transactions that occurs is not dependent on the moment when cash is taken.

expenses are recorded in the same period that the revenues are recognized. Accrual basis gives a clear view of transactions and helps to make sure that revenue earned and the associated expenses that go to that revenue are assessed and accounted for in the same period. Companies use an accrual basis in their accounting in contrast to cashbased basis. Accounting on accrual is a result from implementing the Principle of Matching. Principle.

Additional Paidin Capital (APIC)

A Paidin Capital (APIC) account is where the total amount that was that is paid to purchase a shares of capital, less par value is reported. It's an equity account that is visible as a balance on the Balance Sheet. A different name to describe the account is Capital contributed over the par value.

Amortization

Amortization refers to the procedure of eliminating or liquidating the debt through a sequence of repayments, which include both interest and principal for the lender. It is the process of calculating and the payment plan for repayment of debt using set repayments, in regular installments spread over duration. Most consumers are likely to experience amortization when they take out the purchase of a car or mortgage. It could refer to that the account for the repayments as well as the actual payments.

Amortization may also be the spread out of the capital cost on intangible assets for example, trademarks or patents in a certain amount of duration. It is generally in relation to the asset's expected time of use in taxation and accounting. Amortization is similar in concept to depreciation which is utilized in the case of tangible assets as well as for depletion which can be used in conjunction in conjunction with natural sources. Amortization's purpose is to make sure that an asset matches its expenses to the revenues it earns.

Amortization Schedule

A schedule of amortization of a mortgage includes a table that shows the proportion of interest to the principal for each installment. Every installment has its own mixture of principal and interest. When the payment progresses throughout the calendar, the interest rate decreases while the principal rises in proportion to the overall payment. The total cost remains the same for each month.

Asset

Assets refer to what an organization holds. Assets are defined as with the potential for future economic benefit which are owned or controlled by an organization through previous transactions. Examples of assets are factory, land offices, buildings for office use, machinery automobiles, cashin bank accounts, investment funds such as accounts receivable and intellectual property, such as trademarks, patents and other intellectual property.

Assets are bought and financed with two kinds of obligation which the company incurs in the form of Equity and Liabilities. Both Equity and Liabilities are the funding sources for buy and hold assets.

Balance Sheet

A Balance Sheet can be described as an overview of the financial situation of a business at a particular date. It indicates the total assets minus Total liabilities and Owner's Equity. A Balance Sheet is among the most fundamental financial statements, with the other one being an Income Statement.

Consider a Balance sheet for your home's ownership, and it has the three elements of Liability, Asset and Equity. It is important to note that the Asset is the worth of your home. It is determined through an appraisal. A appraisal considers the recent sale of houses in the vicinity and also compensates for variations such as the amount of bathrooms or bedrooms, the dimensions of the property, etc. The liability refers to the mortgage. It is the amount you have to pay towards the home. The Equity is the amount that's between the value of the Asset as well as the value of the liability. If the value of your house is $200,000 and you carry an outstanding mortgage balance at $150,000, you're left with $50,000 of equity. This is sometimes referred to as homeowner's equity.

If your mortgage debt is greater than the worth of your home, you're being referred to as "upside down" or "under water". Similar principles apply for businesses. If its liabilities exceeds the value of the assets it is considered likely to fail and will eventually go into bankruptcy.

The Books

"Books," or the "books" is a slang broad accounting term that refers to the General Ledger and the various journals maintained by companies. Books can be defined in a sense of a verb that means the recording of a transaction.

Book Value

Book value refers to the amount of an asset in relation to the balance sheet balance. The value of assets is determined by the initial price of the asset minus any amortization, depreciation, or impairment cost incurred against the asset. Book value is the value of net.

Value of books can be different from market value when the asset is worth more when it was in the ownership of another company or has lost value. One example is an office building that is owned by an organization that has grown in value, but it is recorded in the books as expense with depreciation minus. The assets like bonds and stocks probably are of a different worth than the amount they were bought to be sold for.

Capitalize

Capitalization is the process of recording the expense of the asset which will be beneficial in later on rather than take the entire amount and treat it as an expense at the time that it occurs. It's an accounting technique employed to delay the recognition of a major expense, by recording it as a capital asset for the long term. The method of accounting for major expenses more accurately illustrates the scenario. When a company purchases the latest equipment which will last for 10 years, and then a tenth of that cost should be accounted for every year during its operating. Businesses that purchase new equipment with longevity that is longterm can divide the expense for a certain amount of duration. The time frame can be a rough estimate of the life span of the asset in the event that it is helping to generate revenue.

Cash

Coins are currency, as well as check cash, coins and balances of banks accounts. Cash is something we all know is in terms of accounting, however it's the name of the first account under the category of Assets in the Balance Sheet. It is a sum of every bank account in the company and then is calculated from the lowest number on the Cash flow statement. The amount of cash on the bottom of the Cash Flow Statement should be in line to the total of bank account balances.

Cash Flow Statement

Cash flow statements an accounting statement which demonstrates the way that changes to the balance sheet and income statement impact the flow of cash. Cash flow statements splits it down into three parts that include investing, operating and financing.

Common Stock

Common Stock is a type of stock found in every company. Common stock shares provide proof of ownership within an organization. They are the type of shareholders who hold rights to claim the remaining profits and assets of a business after all debts and claims of preferred shareholders are satisfied.

Stockholders who own common stock vote the directors of the corporation at their annual gathering. Common stock gets the share of company profits through dividends. If the company were to be liquidated, secured lenders would receive their money first, then preferred stockholders who are unsecured, lenders who are not followed by common stockholders. When a business is bought and liquidated, the profits go to shareholders following the debts have been paid.

Cost of Goods Sold

Cost of Goods Sold (COGS) is the direct cost that are incurred due to the manufacturing of the products that are sold by companies. It includes the price of materials utilized to create the product as well as the direct labor expenses used in the production of the product. COGS is not inclusive of indirect expenses including distribution cost as well as marketing and sales force expenses. The measurement of COGS is the core of Cost Accounting, which is considered a separate subdiscipline within the accounting field.

Current Assets

Current Assets are the balance sheets that reflect the worth of assets will be converted to cash in the next year. These assets are cash, accounts receivables, stock, marketable securities prepayment of expenses, as well as other assets that are easily transformed into cash. Current assets can be used in the measurement of liquidity in an organization: the speed at which the company is able to convert funds into cash to fund costs and weather a storm.

Debt

It is a debt that must be paid for the amount borrowed. The term "debt" is the generic name for debts, notes, bonds mortgages, debentures, and other similar instruments that act as documents of owed amounts and are accompanied by specific payment dates and timetables. The lender will lend money to the borrower based on an agreement by the borrower that they will pay interest on the debt. Usually, it is with interest due at intervals. The debt is considered a liability to the business (an asset of lenders) and appears in the balance sheet as regardless of the amount that was repayable.

There are numerous varieties and "tiers" of debt based on the repayment terms and schedules as well as the relative seniority of the debts on assets. When bankruptcy is declared, the debt with the highest amount of seniority gets due first as a result of the liquidation process of assets. those with less senior debt will be paid later. The smaller the loan is, the greater the chance of repayment and more interest which investors demand. There are senior and junior, mezzanine as well as convertible debt. Convertible debt is able to convert it into common stock.

Depreciation

The method of depreciation can be that is used to determine the value of tangible assets throughout its life. It's the method of assigning the purchase cost of a product to the time periods when the gains accrue from it. This gives a clearer understanding of the cost on top of the profits they create.

Companies can depreciate assets that are longterm for accounting and tax purposes. Accelerating depreciation could result in greater expense during the early stages as well as shielding the income from tax. Different schedules of depreciation are utilized for various fixed assets. The depreciation schedules vary in terms of length, as well as how quickly depreciation can be incurred. There are techniques for accelerated depreciation which apply greater depreciation to earlier years of the plan.

The term "depreciation" is described as a reduction in value of an asset that is caused by market fluctuations.

Dividend

A dividend is a form of payment that a company makes to its shareholders. It is usually in the form of a dividend distribution. It is usually some of the profit. If a business earns surplus or a profit that it is able to invest into its business. This is known as retained earnings and/or distribute a part from the profits by way of dividends to shareholders. Dividends can be given either in money (a cash dividend) or in stock (a dividend on stock).

Equity

Equity refers to what owners or shareholders of the company have. Equity is the claim of assets. Equity can be defined as owner's equity, also known as shareholder's equity. It is the total value, minus liabilities of the assets of an organization. It's the portion of the equity in assets of an organization that is left after deducting the liabilities. Net assets is the amount between the assets total of the business and all its obligations. Equity is listed on the balance sheet just below the liability line. Be aware of the formula on the balance sheet Equity = Assets + Liabilities Equity.

Imagine this idea with regard to your house and the appraisal value of your home is called the Asset. The mortgage is the Liability and what's in between is the equity. The same is true between these three entities on an accounting balance sheet for a corporation.

Expense

A term is employed to describe the funds that are paid to the company. This includes, for example, paychecks paid to employees and payment to suppliers for products or services, rental electricity bills and supplies. You know the concept.

A different way of thinking about the cost of expenses as a reduction in the equity of the owners due to the use up or evaporation of resources for generating revenues or doing different activities as an element of a company's business.

FASB

FASB refers to the Financial Accounting Standards Board and is a private, independent nongovernmental body responsible that is responsible for establishing generally accepted accounting standards commonly referred to as GAAP in the United States.

Financial Statements and the accounting procedures that generate these statements, should follow these guidelines and standards for them to be considered as true, honest and transparent.

Financial Statements

Financial statements are a set of documents that provide a comprehensive analysis of the financial operations and performance of the company. Three major statement of financials: The Balance Sheet Income Statement and Cash Flow Statement. Each one tells a distinct narrative about the financial performance of an organization. Statements of financials also contain notes to help explain the significance of the financial figures.

Fiscal Year

A fiscal year is the term used to describe a set consisting of twelve consecutive months that is chosen by an organisation as the accounting period it uses to report on its annual financials. A majority of fiscal years are calendar year (January January 1 to December 31) however, a fiscal year may begin and finish anytime during any month. As an example, the majority of U.S. government agencies run an annual fiscal year beginning on October 1 to September 30.

Fixed Asset

A fixed asset can be defined as any item that is tangible and has an effective life span of greater than one calendar year. Fixed assets are factories, offices large equipment, and automobiles. Computers were previously classified as fixed assets however personal computer systems are now priced less than $2,000 and boast life spans that are not much over a year, because the rapid pace technological advancement. Therefore, computer systems are typically costeffective instead of capitalizing as an investment in fixed assets. Fixed assets are longerterm asset that can be found as a fixed asset on the Balance Sheet following the present assets.

GAAP

GAAP refers to Generally Accepted Accounting Principles which are rules, conventions, and processes that must to follow when preparing financial statements. GAAP is the accepted standard for accounting practices within the United States. The principles are developed and supervised by FASB. These include general guidelines as well as specific practices and protocols.

Chapter 7: Income Statement

A Income Statement is a report in summary form which reveals the amount of revenue, expenditures as well as losses or gains over the course of a certain period usually a month, quarter, or even a financial year. The structure of an income statement can be described by: Income Expenses = Income. Net income is often called earnings or profit.

The amount of earnings per share is typically displayed in an income statement. The calculation is done by divising by the Earnings by the total number of shares of stock that are that are outstanding.

Intellectual Property

Intellectual Property (IP) is an asset class that defines and outlines the range of assets that are intangible belonging to a corporation. They are IP assets are protected legally against implementation or use by anyone else without permission. In terms of accounting Intellectual property may include copyrights, patents and trademarks. Intellectual property assets are recorded in the balance sheet, and appraised at the price of acquiring them, minus amortization.

Leverage

Leverage refers to the term used in business to describe the dynamic distinction between two different categories. Two of the most common uses for the word are associated with finance and operations.

Operating leverage is the potential for net income to grow at a greater pace than sales, when there are fixed expenses.

Financial leverage is the usage of longterm debt to obtain funding for an organization. The indicator of financial leverage is called the ratio of equity to debt. It's calculated by the proportion of a company's capital for loans (debt) against the worth of its shares (equity) or debt/equity. Financial leverage increases the risk of companies since debt repayments remain constant and revenue or sales can fluctuate but not enough to pay for debt.

Liability

The term "liability" refers to the obligation to make a specific sum at a specific date in exchange for a present or past advantage. It's what a business has to repay. This includes, for example, loans tax, payables, or the longterm debt resulting due to a bond issue.

On the balance sheet, liabilities are classified as either Current due to be paid in the financial year, or Long Term, which will be paid later in the near future.

Line of Credit

A line of credit an agreement with a financial institution typically a bank, and customers for borrowing shortterm at the point of need. The customer can draw from the credit line anytime, however it can not exceed the maximum limit specified in the arrangement. The line of credit (LOC) is like a credit card. It's intended to reduce the requirement for operational funds in order to pay charges and other obligations for current assets, such as accounts receivable and inventory have a difficult time turning into cash.

Liquidity

Liquidity is the ability of cash or close liquid cash sources, such as the marketable securities that can be used to fulfill the company's obligations. The measurement of liquidity or the capacity of current assets to satisfy the requirements of current liabilities is known as the current ratio. Current ratios are derived from current assets minus current liabilities. Current assets comprise inventory that isn't as easy to quickly convert to cash.

Quick ratio is an additional measure to determine the easiest liquidated portion of assets and obligations. It's used to assess the extent to which a company has assets that could be turned into cash to pay expenses. Current assets comprised in the quick ratio include money, marketable securities in addition to accounts receivable. Inventory isn't part of the calculation, as it's hard to liquidate rapidly without incurring a substantial loss. Quick ratios are an excellent indicator over the present ratio of capability of a business to meet its obligations immediately as it removes inventory from the calculations.

Marktomarket

Marktomarket refers to the process employed to define the accounting of fair values. It is a method of taking into account what is the "fair value" of an item or liability, based on the price at which it is traded or another objectively assessed value. Fair value accounting is included in Generally Accepted Accounting Principles (GAAP) in the United States since the early 1990s.

Net Income (loss)

Net income (or the loss) is the total amount a company earned or lost during the duration of. It's the sum of all gains and revenues during a time period, minus all expenses and losses during the time. This is the lowest number on the income Statement as well as the highest figure of the Cash Flow Statement. For calculating net income subtract total revenue from the total expense. Net income is also known as earnings or profit.

P & L responsibility

P&L refers to the profit and loss report also known as income statement. P & L responsibility is one of the primary tasks of any executive. This involves monitoring and ultimately judging the net earnings before expenses of the entire department. The performance of the executive is based by financial performance. Executives have direct control in the way resources of the company are distributed and the strategies are designed to execute plan.

Financial statements for internal use must be created to assess the performance of an executive that is accountable for P&L charge.

Par Value

Par value represents the amount that is shown on the face of the security. Par value accounts are an equity stock account that is shown as a balance Sheet. The par value for stock accounts is used to track the number of shares that are outstanding. Par value is an amount of money that is that is assigned to every share. It's an undetermined value, but typically $.01

Par value can also be a word used to refer to the amount of face value for bonds. Many bonds have their initial value, or par value of 1,000 dollars. When interest rates change during the duration that the bonds are issued, their price can be calculated in terms of an increase in discount or a percentage or par value. This is the way bonds offer yields that differ from the fixed rate when they are issued.

Preferred Stock

Preferred Stock is one of the classes of shares that have the right to earn income or acquire assets following bondholders, but prior to common shareholders. The preferred stock is also able to receive special treatment for dividends. Stockholders who have preferred stock will receive dividends prior to common stockholders get dividends. Sometimes, these dividends are made in stock, rather than cash. The preferred stock may also have the possibility of being converted to ordinary stock.

Principal

Principal is the term used to describe the principal amount in the loan. It's the initial amount that is lent or invested. Most bonds have a principal that is held until it is paid fully at the conclusion of the period that the bond has. When loans are amortized, such as mortgages, both interest and principal are repaid with each payment. This payment schedule as well as the portion that includes principal and interest is known as the amortization table.

Retained Earnings

Retained earnings refers to the proportion of income that is that is not distributed as dividends but instead retained by the business to invest in its primary business, or used to repay its debt. The earnings are recorded as shareholders equity on the balance sheet. It is calculated as equity of the owners less capital contributed.

Revenue

The term "revenue" refers to funds that are taken by a business typically through sales. It's a monetary measurement of the services or products sold. The Revenue line is the highest in the income Statement.

SEC

Securities and Exchange Commission, an agency that was authorized by U.S. Congress to regulate financial markets, and in particular accounting practices for publicly traded corporations. The website of the agency is www.sec.gov

Shares Outstanding

shares outstanding is the total amount of stock owned by a company owned by its shareholders, as well as restricted shares held by employees and officers of the. The outstanding shares appear in a balance sheet of a company in the section "Capital Stock." The amount of shares outstanding is utilized to calculate key indicators like a firm's market capitalization (the share price x shares outstanding) in addition to the profits per share (Earnings/shares outstanding).

Stock

Shares, also known as stock is the generic expression used to define the ownership certificates issued by the company. Stocks are an investment tool or vehicle to invest in equity. Every share of stock is a portion of the ownership stake within the firm.

Chapter 8: Awareness Of The Financial Literation

"If you don't know the meaning of money, and do not own a financial institution that's a sign you're an economic slave. - John Hope Bryant, CEO, Operation HOPE

The majority of individuals of today are living in a state of confusion. It is a struggle to achieve top marks in high school, attend the college of our choice and hope to graduate with distinction, land an excellent job in an eminent company, marry, have kids and be sure that you go through the same pattern. In all these years but we don't think about accumulating the financial knowledge we need. It is because we're attracted to earning good incomes or spend money to display our extravagant lifestyle we've earned from studying at a high level at school, and making sure we meet the requirements of our children (family members as well) and also a small amount to prepare for retirement.

It's an ideal time to stop the cycle. Rethink the way you think. Instead of working for a well-known firm, consider being a part of one. Instead of salary, consider the possibility of owning stocks. Also, you can expand your world of possibilities by becoming economically smart.

A person who is financially educated is one who is aware of how money works and the way you handle the money, invest it and grow the amount. Wikipedia describes financial literacy as a collection of knowledge and skills that help individuals make smart decisions with all of their money resources.

There are the various aspects of finance, and learn about various strategies for managing cash. Learn about the advantages of giving to charitable causes.

In nations like Singapore, Canada, the United States and other countries in which the government is devoted to teaching its citizens the best ways to handle their finances. Although this may not be common in all nations however, it would be an important step in the right direction should this plan be applied globally.

Financial literacy is crucial.

A discussion about being financially educated is not enough, so I've decided to write down the essentials of this notion to help us comprehend the many benefits available to us.

Equipment for knowledge with the correct expertise and knowledge, you will quickly learn when and how to make investments. Also, you'll learn to navigate the world which is more about the spending aspect rather than savings or investing.

Financial management that is effective Youth today have access to credit cards prior to leaving high school. However, they don't know the impact of compound interest against the cards. The financial education process will lower the chance of dropping out of school in young kids and will enable them to be successful in the society.

Make the right financial choices If you're financially knowledgeable, you will be able to take the correct decisions that will protect your financial security.

Maximizing Success: One is able to achieve accomplishment, but having a solid financial foundation can certainly boost your chances of chances of success and place you at the highest.

In order to eliminate debt, financial knowledge will allow us to eliminate all debt and can also ease the financial burden on us.

Although you've learned about the significance to financial knowledge, that it's not enough. The goal must be to have it. Make sure you are aware of the financial market. Schedule an appointment with a financial broker. Purchase some shares. Making the right choice of investment may be challenging, but it is important to realize that it requires an enormous amount of time and energy on your behalf to develop a financial savvy. It is essential to learn everything you can about investing and accounting and also be prepared to alter how you think. Implement new ways of thinking that are the focus of the coming chapters. Implementing these habits will aid you to achieve financial security.

Chapter 9: Habits For Successful

Being successful is a common aspiration and they are always looking at new methods to become extremely prosperous. While doing this many people do not realize that they can achieve success within themselves. Habits are a key factor in the success of a person. The majority of our behavior is influenced by our the habits we have developed. Your current level of success and what you can achieve in the coming years largely depend on the habits you have. Establishing healthy habits and a positive outlook helps anyone achieve success with time.

Since the beginning of time humans have been studied by many philosophers and thought leaders to find how to be successful. Research has proven that the most successful people have developed positive practices from very early stage of their life. Below are seven of the essential habits that make successful individuals. If you are looking to become successful, you should change these habits within your own life, and remain constant.

i. Aim-oriented

The very first step to success is becoming determined. Be consistent when making goals and commitments, as well as to working from clear written goals on a every day basis in order to organize your daily activities. The most successful individuals are very goal-driven. They have a clear idea of the things they would like to achieve and often write it down. they've written down a plan to achieve it, and they're both reviewing and reworking their strategies every day. Also, you should try to establish good habits that allow you that will help you achieve your objectives.

ii. Results-driven

The other characteristic of effective people is being driven by results. This is accomplished through two methods.

First, you must practice the art of continual learning, so that you become better at what you are doing.

Another method is one of managing time. It means you establish clearly defined priorities for the things you are doing and concentrate on the best utilization you can make of the time.

Every successful person is focused on achieving their goals.

iii. Action-oriented

The 3rd important habit you need to create is the habit of taking constant actions.

It's the most crucial factor for accomplishment. It's a way to start and complete the task swiftly. The key is to maintain and develop the sense of urgency, as well as the ability to take action. The speed at which you work in everything you are doing is crucial for your success.

To overcome the urge to delay and put aside your worries and dedicate yourself towards achieving your top targets. A combination of goal-orientation, results-orientedness and action-orientation will definitely result in great results by its own right.

It is highly recommended that you learn the use of SMART goals. They help you set achievable goals you are able to track and measure.

iv. People-oriented

The fourth thing you should consider is the orientation of people.

That's where you place relations at the forefront of your existence. It is your choice to develop in you the values of patience empathy, kindness and compassion. A large portion of your joy is derived from the ability you have to interact easily with people.

It's a good thing that you are able to become an excellent person to be with other people when you choose to make the effort.

According to what Aristotle stated, the sole method of learning an habit is to do the habit regularly. When you are able to practice becoming an excellent human being within your interactions with other people as well as the more you learn the qualities you have learned and eventually become this person.

Becoming more relaxed with people who surround you is an effective method to promote a positive way of life.

V. A healthy lifestyle

Fifth habit which highly successful individuals are able to develop is awareness of their health.

It is important to keep an check on your eating habits and consuming the appropriate food items in appropriate portions. It is essential to work out regularly to use each joint and muscle in your body in order to stay healthy and agile. In addition, you should maintain a healthy routine of relaxation and rest that together exercising and diet, can help you live the rest of your life in a good condition.

Be aware that your health is the single most crucial item you own, and is largely dependent on your lifestyle choices with regard to how you live your life.

vi. Fair

Sixth habit is one of integrity and honesty.

In the end, the persona you create as you progress through life is much more crucial more than just about everything else.

Honesty implies that you follow an "principle of reality" in all you do. You're completely honest with your self as well as with those surrounding you. You define very clearly the goals for yourself, and arrange your life around these beliefs. Develop a vision of your life and follow your path in line of your highest standards. It is your duty to never compromise your integrity or your peace of mind to whatever or whomever.

Honesty is essential to embracing all the good habits that you're forming.

vii. Self-discipline

The seventh and final habit, as well as the sole habit that can guarantee the others is one of self-control.

The ability to manage yourself, to manage yourself in a controlled manner is one of the greatest qualities you'll ever acquire as an individual. Self-control can be correlated with achievement in any area of your life.

If you're in need of a bit of assistance to remain motivated in your quest to live the life you've always dreamed of Check out these inspirational successful quotes.

Each of these behaviors, such as goals-oriented, results-oriented, focused, people-oriented, healthy in fairness and discipline, are possible to develop. The place you're at as well as what you're today due to your actions. The habits you have developed are mostly by accident, since the moment you were an infant.

Now, you have the ability to have complete control over your development of personal characteristics and your character as well as all that will happen for you into the near future when you make the choice immediately to discover your own definition of the behaviors that can lead to the highest level of achievement.

If you can develop the same positive habits many successful individuals are able to achieve, you can be able to enjoy the same success. Your possibilities are unlimited.

Chapter 10: Steps To Get Rich

The secret to becoming truly wealthy in life aren't secret. They're well known. Yet, regardless of how acknowledged but they're certainly not a norm. A large portion of the people in the world and a significant portion of every country are completely in contrast with these supposedly secret methods of making money.

But, if you're determined about the future of your riches, you're following the wisdom passed down the centuries. Although it is largely unnoticed by the majority of individuals, it was used throughout time by people who are among the most successful and most wealthy people.

i. Live under your means.

The most famous method of making money is living under your feet.

Translation? Do not spend more than you make. Time period. Yet, not many adhere to this suggestion. Most are focused on spending more than they could. It could be to have having the illusion that they are wealthier than they have been, or for some different reason, it is the reality in a lot of the world's developed countries.

Actually the majority of Americans reported that they are breaking even or spending more than they earn every month, as per an investigation conducted by the Pew Charitable Trusts, which made its conclusions on the basis of responses from more than 7,000 American households.

ii. Take 20 percent off your earnings.

A similar survey conducted by the Pew Charitable Trusts found that three-quarters of Americans do not have any savings whatsoever. However, to be wealthy it is necessary to put aside minimum 20 percent of the income you earn from the highest levels. Everybody has heard it before however how many adhere to this rule?

The phrase "pay yourself first" carries significant weight in this case. While some don't find the importance in this, others realize that this provides not only a rainy day fund in an emergency, but also moment-of-the-opportunity cash. If the perfect opportunity comes it, you'll need cash to take advantage of the opportunity. If you're not able to raise enough money, you've have missed out on the opportunity.

A different study revealed that almost fifty percent of Americans don't have savings in retirement. In addition, nearly 70% of Americans do not have more than $1,000 in savings which is a small moment away from a complete, complete meltdown of their money.

iii. Maintain a detailed record of your expenditures.

What's the next step in becoming riches? Be vigilant about every penny you make. This is not only for the large expenditures. Each expense must be tracked using the aid of a fine-toothed broach. Benjamin Franklin once said, "Beware of small expenses. A small leak will sink a large ship."

Although it might seem to be to not pay attention to the small details, in essence when you are focusing your self with details, the more successful you'll become. You can cancel your gym membership that you've not utilized in the last the past six months. You can get rid of the expensive television subscription. Get rid of expensive drinks and dining out in the event that you aren't able to pay for it.

Install an app or purchase a notebook that is small and record every expenditure, regardless of how it is big or small. Find and track the costs by using the software that is widely available. Find out how your money is being spent. How much would you be able to spend every month to save money that could otherwise go to waste?

iv. Eliminate bad debts.

I'm not saying that all debt is bad, but there are many debts that are not good. Certain debts are an excellent credit to hold. Others, like high interest credit card balances or loans with very excessive interest, are considered to be bad loans. The goal is to clear of any poor loans. This is particularly true when you pay only the regular monthly installments.

There is no way to be riches in your life if consume a significant portion of your earnings on the interest on funds you've already used. Use the credit or loan that is the most expensive and increase the minimum payment until the loan is fully paid. Next, you can move on and on to the next. Next. Till it's gone.

If you're free of bad loans (not those with good credit, like real estate investment mortgages or the loans you need to expand the business of yours, for instance) you can take that cash and put it into your savings. You should not invest and make money for the holidays or purchasing a new car after you've been debt-free. Keep your eyes on the prize.

V. Have the roof on your head.

Most people's largest investment is house. The portion of the world leases its houses. Although temporary employment is fine If you're committed to your financial goals it is essential to be able to afford a shelter you need. Renting doesn't guarantee you riches over night, but when you lease you can pay for the mortgage of someone else. Actually, it makes another person rich.

If you have to no matter how much you require to reduce your lifestyle take whatever steps you need to for a house. Get in touch with a mortgage agent to assess your current situation. Make a list of your targets and develop an strategy.

If you don't have enough cash to pay for a downpayment to this point then you must find out the steps to purchase your first home. It's not about the dream house you've always wanted to live in. But, in the long run the funds you spend on your mortgage is likely to be invested far more efficiently than the cash used to pay rent.

vi. Decimate your bad habits.

Unhealthy habits hinder us from reaching a variety of targets. They hinder our bodies in losing weight earning more money, saving more, investing, and so on. The only way to truly succeed in your life is to break the harmful practices. The only way to get ahead is to eliminate those bad habits before they can lead you to an unending downward spiral.

It's difficult to accomplish things that require a lot of your time and effort, such as making it rich, without getting rid of those bad habits first. It's not only about poor financial practices as well as every other habit that impacts your physical, emotional, or psychologically.

Evidently, the path to success doesn't only mean removing those bad habits that keep us back. It's to ensure that we implement several of the most effective habits in our lives and best techniques for business that virtually ensure your future performance and improvements by autopilot.

vii. Create daily targets.

Achieving wealth is a huge objective. It isn't enough to claim that you'd like to become rich. In the first place you must have an exact amount and need a precise date for when you hit it. This is the larger picture. To complement that larger image, it is important to create goals for yourself every single day.

The daily goal setting process helps you set milestones that will help you reach your greater objectives. Break down the goal in realistic daily goals that do not appear to be too overwhelming. If, for instance, you're hoping to reach an estimated net worth of 10 million in the coming five or ten years, determine what you have to do each day for you to achieve the desired goal.

It's obvious that it's difficult to reach that big aim of becoming wealthy if you're starting from the ground or, even more so. But compound interest can be extremely powerful and, even if you fail to achieve your goal it is possible to use any money that you earn and use it in smart investment choices that will yield excellent returns.

viii. Manage your time effectively.

All of us have the exact amount of time to spend in the world. It's not like you possess more time than one person. And that individual doesn't have more time. If they're a great politician, business magnate or famous athlete they're not in a better position than you do. The greatest equalizer is time in this world.

The most important thing, however, is the way in which our time is utilized. The precious hours of our day life can be easily wasted. It is impossible to earn money by wasting precious time in pursuits that are not worth your while. Make sure you manage your time effectively with a well-planned and efficient time management system in order to keep you on course to meet your objectives.

ix. Create enormous value.

Any strategy that you employ for making cash (online as well as offline) but without delivering massive sums of money, as well as doing it continuously throughout time, there's very little chance of making it wealthier. The people who have contributed the greatest value to this globe have made the biggest fortunes.

It is a fact that one of the fundamental concepts of success says that you must put in the greatest effort to earn the lowest initial profit. If you're seeking methods to make wealthy quickly, or with little effort, you'll most likely be unsuccessful.

The issue? There are many unethical marketers out there in search of a easy solution. But, that's not the case. If you're hoping to be wealthy, you need to increase the value of your assets by a huge amount in order to always do this over the course of time.

x. Develop many sources of income passively.

Any person who is looking to become serious must create several sources of income that are passive. The importance of passive income is immense for accumulating wealth. It is essential to earn income automatically if you wish to have a large net worth.

There are many ideas for passive income generating methods which you can try. The most well-known include real estate, and dividend income, for those who can pay for the typically high cost hurdles to enter these sectors. Some choose to earn income from a passive source by starting an online blog, creating digital goods like books or courses, or developing online courses among others.

Whatever you choose to focus on, if you are concentrating solely on passive earnings, you complete your job one time and are regularly paid. In contrast, active income demands the constant commitment of time and effort to generate income. When you stop working, you cease making. It is impossible to boost your wealth or earnings by producing an active source of income. Make sure you are earning passive income to see your wealth grow exponentially in the course of the course of.

xi. Make sure you invest in the things that you are familiar with.

If you truly would like to make a fortune then you must put your money into what you are familiar with. If, for instance, you are employed in the pharmaceutical sector, don't look to get into a farming company. Do you understand the concept? Make investments in the things you are familiar with. If you are knowledgeable about the effects of drugs, you should become involved in biotechnology.

The more you are aware of the subject or area The more likely you will be able to come up with ways to make massive amounts of cash to you in the near future. Nobody else can help you with this. When you make a decision to decide to invest in something that you are familiar with ensure that you adhere to the rules strictly.

It's fine to place all your eggs into the same basket as you like, so it's as long as you observe the eggs like a hawk. When you become lost in your thoughts or lose focus and lose interest, the situation will go to hell. Take note of this if intend to treat your money seriously.

xii. Be mindful of your own work.

If you are able to make money when you work as an employee however, it's far more challenging. It is better to create your own company and be involved. Your heart and all your soul to the venture and keep striving to improve it even if it doesn't work out. Even if you don't succeed regardless of whether it occurs frequently, you can learn from those successes and progress.

Henry Ford learned a lot from his failures, yet didn't quit. When he declared bankruptcy once, and then was forced to quit his first company but he did not throw his towel in the ring. He worked hard at his company. Each successful entrepreneur has had to fail. The reason they achieved success at such an enormous scale was that they refused to quit.

Chapter 11: Think Thoroughly Prior To Deciding On A Career

If you're about to finish your degree or are just about to choose a field you're scared of to not know exactly what it is you'd like to accomplish in your future.

The fear is magnified in the sense that everybody else is trying to pressure that you choose to pursue a particular career.

If you're struggling and do not know how to begin in deciding on the right career path, don't be all on your own. Help is on the way!

Breathe deeply and take a look at our top 10 ideas for choosing a profession.

i. Learn your preferred work fashion

The way you work influences the way you perform in certain professions.

If, for instance, you're someone who is prone to be a procrastinator, a position that you are directly accountable to someone else is likely to be better as opposed to a position in which you're left completely on your own most of the time.

Consider the positions that you've had in the past.

Which areas were you successful in, and what ones were you struggling in? Do you like having the ability to set your own work schedule and operate in your own way? Do you require someone to make you accountable?

There are of course many other elements that impact the performance of your job. However, your work style is a major factor.

ii. Identify your skills

Every job requires a unique collection of competencies. Sales managers require exceptional abilities to lead and teachers need to be able to effectively communicate with parents and students.

Spend the time to discover your strengths and weaknesses. Make a list of all strengths and abilities you have even if they don't look like it will help you to find an employment.

The ability to master every skill you possess even those that do not look particularly appealing - can aid you in finding a profession that you love and are proficient in.

As an example, being skilled in video games might appear to be an unproven talent. But dig a little deeper.

What are you skilled with when it comes down to playing video games? Problem solving? Creative? Decision?

These are crucial abilities that are applicable to many different career paths.

iii. Establish your objectives

What is your dream your career?

Are you looking to assist others? Are you looking to travel? How much do you wish to earn?

If you're working towards a job which isn't in line with the long-term objectives you have It's likely that you'll never feel satisfied.

The goals of course change as time passes, and the items that once were extremely crucial are no longer so. Still, it is beneficial to know the goals you'd like to achieve so you know what goals to strive toward.

iv. Learn to recognize your beliefs

Out of all the suggestions to choose a profession contemplating the things you want from the work you do is among the most crucial.

Do you like working alone or do you want to be social all day to be satisfied?

Do you want to spend time with your loved ones and return in your home by a certain time every day? Do you feel comfortable being able to work overtime, and then being more flexible in your schedule?

Think about these issues and avoid careers that do not meet the values you cherish most.

V. Do the mathematics

Also, you will need to calculate your costs and consider how much time and cash it'll require to get you there you'd like to go.

How many years of schooling are you required to pursue the career you want? Are you prepared and willing to put in the effort and resources required?

vi. Be aware that things could change

There are a lot of "Best Careers" lists that suggest you must strive for the right job since it's guaranteed to bring an sum.

There isn't a solution to completely guarantee job the security and stability. It is possible that there will be lots of job seekers in the present, but what will it be like the next 10 years?

It's not necessary to disregard predictions regarding the future prospects for your particular position. However, don't choose a job only because it's in a listing somewhere.

Changes can happen over time and the top job may not be even on the radar in just a few years.

vii. Speak to those who are working in the area

A conversation with someone who is working in the area you're thinking about can prove highly beneficial. If you have the opportunity to talk with multiple individuals, it's better.

A fifteen minute interview could provide a wealth of information about a particular career.

You can ask questions regarding the benefits and drawbacks of the position, including what they would prefer they were able to go back to the present, and which qualities they considered to be the most beneficial.

The job shadowing process can be as, if perhaps as beneficial.

Being able to follow someone's story for a day can be like catching the glimpse of your future. You'll get an impression of whether you would like to perform exactly the same thing as the person you are following, and this can aid in deciding on the future of your career.

viii. Think about an internship

A job internship can be another method for you to experience hands-on work to determine whether a specific career path is the right one for you. There's nothing more practical than completing the job that you dream of dedicating your entire life to!

Internships can assist you in getting your foot into the doors of an organization you'd like to join. A study found that 52% of interns get given a permanent job with the firm they were working for!

ix. Make use of the resources you have available

If you're currently at college, you probably will have a relationship with an advisor to careers who will assist you in deciding which profession is the most suitable for you. A counselor is able to provide advice on choosing the right career, assist you to find internships, and connect you with a person to talk to or be a shadow.

There are numerous sites that could assist you in narrowing the options. This blog, for instance, offers a wealth of info for those who are trying to decide on the right career.

x. Be agile

If you've spent a significant amount of money and time learning for a certain profession, it may be difficult to acknowledge that you're really not keen on it.

Some people feel discontented with being on an occupation simply because they don't want to be a victim of their time invested in preparing.

Chapter 12: Determinable Goals

My philosophy is different from the norm concerning goal setting. It is my belief that when you employ those who are right for you (winners) and they are naturally desire to be successful. They aren't motivators in themselves. They are tools that helps winners evaluate the progress they make, and to adjust their path and, once they have achieved them be proud of their accomplishments.

This is my view on why the importance of goals is:

Find out when you've won:Goals gives those who are eligible to feel the satisfaction of satisfaction when they achieve or beat the goals they set.

Self-improvement: Goals provide you with an opportunity to review and make improvements when not doing things the way you want to be.

Make winning a habit: Winning is infectious. Set achievable goals. It is a huge benefit when teams exceed their objectives.

The first two reasons are simple. Let me discuss the third motive in greater depth.

Some companies think having goals that are far reaching is the most effective way in order to encourage people to accomplish more. Personally, I don't believe in the idea. I think that winners are excessively ambitious and are likely to have goals that are overly ambitious in the beginning. Also, if you select the right individuals (that's an essential aspect to consider here) You can adopt another approach when it comes towards goal setting.

I believe it's important to establish goals that can be achieved. This is a fascinating thing. It's been my experience that if the "very achievable" goal is 10, and I make the person to set their goal at 11 (hoping that I can provide myself with some buffer so that they can get up to 10) the result is nine. If I establish the goal based on 9 winners, the winner will get 10 more often than they do. If the rest of her group is similarly on the path to hitting 10 points, the majority of that group will get 11 points. It's counterintuitive, right? It's actually not.

People who win want to be winners. They feed off it. They get extremely competitive after they are successful and achieve great results when they're focused and confident. But, I believe that the winners have a lot of emotion. If they are successful, they inspire everyone around them. However, when they lose they have the reverse impact. It is easy to fall down if you aren't quite at their goals.

If you are setting goals for financial success it can be more challenging to be able to count on this approach. If I'm hoping to achieve 500 million dollars and set my goal for $ 450 million. It's possible to think that I'm putting $ 50 million unaccounted for but I'm not giving enough motive to outperform and charging people excessively to achieve results that are not simple to attain. This has been proved many times over the years that employing the right employees by setting a goal of $ 450 million, it will earn us an amount of 500 million. When I decided to decided to set my goal at $ 5 million that I fell short. The process requires patience, discipline as well as a great deal of trust and it's a great idea, but it's actually effective.

Chapter 13: Give Yourself Time

Do you ever feel overwhelmed, rushed and feeling stressed, anxious or overwhelmed? Many of us such as myself, these emotions are commonplace particularly in the present. Even though we feel that there's not enough time, or that our lives have become too overwhelming is common for many of us, it's not a new thing but it is becoming a common occurrence across our world today particularly as we discover ourselves "stuck". In "all the time - laptops, cell phones, Blackberries, iPhones and more."

Unfortunately, a lot people allow themselves to get caught up in our routines as well as our equipment for communication and our coworkers, our family members, customers as well as our work schedules along with others "demands" and "responsibilities" of our lives. While some of these are essential and lots are in need of our attention, often we overlook that we are those who created our lives in the manner we are and let us to become exhausted, overwhelmed and caught by our endless to-do lists .

Below are some ideas you can think about and do in your quest to increase your capacity to enjoy more space and time within your daily life:

i. Pay attention to your time-related relationship the schedule you have set, as well as your obligations.

What do you think of the clock? What are your thoughts about your timetable? Do you feel like a victim to your responsibilities in your home, work or in general? If you are able to admit to yourself your feelings about issues you must address in your daily life, the better it is to alter your attitude (if you'd prefer to change). The majority of us suffer from a spooky or numb relation to time. Take a look at some of the bizarre things we think of saying: "Time flies." "I never have enough time to do what I want to do." "Where did the time go?" The above and other statements or thoughts make us the victim of a victim when it comes to time and obligation to it.

ii. Say "no" to things.

It can be a challenge for a lot of us. The life trainer and writer Cheryl Richardson says, "If it's not an absolute 'yes,' then it's a 'no." Sometimes we need a little help or advice from other people on the subject. However, being able to say no to any requests or invitations that we get is a crucial part of making sure we have some time and more space. In addition, looking over the numerous tasks we're juggling in our lives at present and the ability to eliminate the majority of them (by disconnection) is also essential. It's not about being a jerk or unreliable, it's about realizing the things we can and cannot accomplish. Our "disease to please" causes us to answer "yes" to things that are really something we should say "no" to.

iii. You should allow yourself longer that you think you'll need.

When we cram our lives and weeks, our schedules and task lists with too much and tasks, we could be overwhelmed and fail. Most of the time it is not even apparent the length of time it takes to accomplish basic tasks or projects. While I'm learning that trying to accomplish multiple things within a limited amount of time is detrimental to the work itself, the other people who is involved, as well as my personal feelings of wellbeing and tranquility throughout the entire process. Would it be better if we had ample time to complete our projects as well as get around and organize items? Imagine how it would feel for the people around us. Also, think about how much more innovative and enthusiastic, in love with and efficient we would be during the course of our work.

In order to do this, seek help, feedback, and guidance from people whom you trust, from friends who are familiar with you as well as from people that seem to be enjoying some peace within their lives. You don't need to solve this problem by ourselves. Everything all around us is speeding. Expectations and requirements put on us can be (and sometimes appear to be) absurd.

Chapter 14: Consistency Is The Key To Success

Consistency is the most important factor to achievement. Habits are formed through consistency. The actions we perform every day. The actions we take lead to our the success we desire. In the words of Anthony Robbins said, "It's not just what we do once in a while that defines our lives. What we consistently do is what we do. "

This implies that you work the equivalent of 3-4 hours per day focused work on Launch School materials. There is no way to do it all at once, so put aside any attempts. You can turn off Facebook, Skype, mobile phone and instruct your partner or parents not to interrupt your.

It's going to be tough to do so, and even more challenging once the initial excitement and excitement wears off. It's easy to start making excuses. It could be that a whole time without studying for a while, only to return the next day, and so on and so on until finally you give up. Be careful not to let this happen you. Don't be a quitter. It's not your fault. Set a goal and stick to it and you'll reach your goal in the final. It could take up to a one year or two years of consistent effort, but it can yield positive outcomes.

How can we be consistent?

If you don't stick to a consistent approach and consistent, it will be impossible to get off. What is important is being consistent with what you'd like to become If at any time you're working towards the goal, something occurs which stops your from working towards it regularly. It is likely that you will fail time repeatedly, and you'll be disappointed and defeated If you're constant in your efforts and do the best you could to achieve it Only then will you get it done.

The initial stages of a business plan can be a failure if it isn't consistent It's crucial to remain consistent with running your business.

i. Consistency makes you relevant

There must be a regular workflow in your job. Being consistent can be dangerous for those around you. What you do you're trying to remain current, and you do not want to hear that people will say that you're irrelevant. The reason consistency is important is because it ensures you are pertinent when you go back each day with the exact goals you set at the beginning of your day. Over time, people are likely to start taking your work seriously, and perceive you in a different way.

ii. Constance in actions

The fact that you are consistent in your actions doesn't necessarily mean that you repeat the same things repeatedly. It's about developing, growing and gaining the most value from what you're doing. Make use of new concepts in your work and be creative when you work.

The goal isn't doing something and not looking at the outcome and knowing whether it had any impact.

It's not all about excellence. It's all about perseverance. Work that is consistent and hard-working leads to the success you desire. The best will be achieved "

If you achieve your goal the brain releases an increase in dopamine, the body's pleasure chemical that make you feel happy, warm and confident to face every challenge life has to provide. The reason we want to achieve success is because of the adrenaline rush it provides feeling of having our name recognized and loved and the feeling of joy that comes with seeing your name engraved on a monument while crowds of people cheer you on. Being successful makes us feel content and happiness is the goal that defines your life.

The success of your life is contingent on the amount of effort you put into it, or in some instances it's about how fortunate you are. This motivates athletes to push the limits of their abilities and encourages scientists to devote hours to the research, and it motivates people in business to think of an innovative and new idea. The success of a person is what propels the world forward. It is the common fire that fuels the human race. It was important to people in the past. it's important to us today, and will be vital to every one of us in the years to be.

www.ingramcontent.com/pod-product-compliance
Lightning Source LLC
Chambersburg PA
CBHW071441080526
44587CB00014B/1941